IS-703.A: NIMS Resource Management

By

Fema

1/15/2010

Lesson 1:

Resource Management Overview

What Is NIMS?

Each day communities respond to numerous emergencies. Most often, these incidents are managed effectively at the local level.

However, there are some incidents that may require a collaborative approach that includes personnel from:

- Multiple jurisdictions,
- A combination of specialties or disciplines,
- Several levels of government,
- Nongovernmental organizations, and
- The private sector.

The National Incident Management System, or NIMS, provides the foundation needed to ensure that we can work together when our communities and the Nation need us the most.

NIMS integrates best practices into a comprehensive, standardized framework that is flexible enough to be applicable across the full spectrum of potential incidents, regardless of cause, size, location, or complexity.

Using NIMS allows us to work together to prepare for, prevent, respond to, recover from, and mitigate the effects of incidents.

Presidential Directives

- HSPD-5 identified steps for improved coordination in response to incidents. It required the Department of Homeland Security (DHS) to coordinate with other Federal departments and agencies and State, local, and tribal governments to establish a National Response Framework (NRF) and a National Incident Management System (NIMS).
- Presidential Policy Directive 8 (PPD-8) describes the Nation's approach to preparedness-one that involves the whole community, including individuals, businesses, community- and faith-based organizations, schools, tribes, and all levels of government (Federal, State, local, tribal and territorial). Click on this link to view PPD-8.

NIMS and NRF

NIMS provides a systematic, proactive approach to guide departments and agencies at all levels of government, nongovernmental organizations, and the private sector to work seamlessly to prevent, protect against, respond to, recover from, and mitigate the effects of incidents, regardless of cause, size, location, or complexity, in order to reduce the loss of life and property and harm to the environment.

The NRF is a guide to how the Nation conducts all-hazards response—from the smallest incident to the largest catastrophe. This key document establishes a comprehensive, national, all-hazards approach to domestic incident response. The Framework identifies the key response principles, roles and structures that organize national response. It describes how communities, States, the Federal Government, and private-sector and nongovernmental partners apply these principles for a coordinated, effective national response.

NIMS Components

NIMS is much more than just using the Incident Command System or an organization chart.
NIMS is a consistent, nationwide, systematic approach that includes the following components:

- Preparedness
- Communications and Information Management
- Resource Management
- Command and Management
- Ongoing Management and Maintenance

The components of NIMS were not designed to stand alone, but to work together.

Preparedness

Actions taken to plan, organize, equip, train, and exercise to build and sustain the capabilities necessary to prevent, protect against, mitigate the effects of, respond to, and recover from those threats that pose the greatest risk. Within NIMS, preparedness focuses on the following elements: planning; procedures and protocols; training and exercises; personnel qualifications, licensure, and certification; and equipment certification.

Communications and Information Management

Emergency management and incident response activities rely on communications and information systems that provide a common operating picture to all command and coordination sites. NIMS describes the requirements necessary for a standardized framework for communications and emphasizes the need for a common operating picture. This component is based on the concepts of interoperability, reliability, scalability, and portability, as well as the resiliency and redundancy of communications and information systems.

Resource Management

Resources (such as personnel, equipment, or supplies) are needed to support critical incident objectives. The flow of resources must be fluid and adaptable to the requirements of the incident. NIMS defines standardized mechanisms and establishes the resource management process to identify requirements, order and acquire, mobilize, track and report, recover and demobilize, reimburse, and inventory resources.

Command and Management

The Command and Management component of NIMS is designed to enable effective and efficient incident management and coordination by providing a flexible, standardized incident management structure. The structure is based on three key organizational constructs: the Incident Command System, Multiagency Coordination Systems, and Public Information.

Ongoing Management and Maintenance

Within the auspices of Ongoing Management and Maintenance, there are two components: the National Integration Center (NIC) and Supporting Technologies.

What Is NIMS Resource Management?

During an incident, getting the right resources, to the right place, at the right time, can be a matter of life and death.

NIMS establishes a standardized approach for managing resources before, during, and after an incident.

Resources include:

- Personnel,
- Equipment,
- Supplies, and

- Facilities.

Prior to an incident, resources are inventoried and categorized by kind and type, including their size, capacity, capability, skills, and other characteristics.

Mutual aid partners exchange information about resource assets and needs. Resource readiness and credentialing are maintained through periodic training and exercises.

When an incident occurs, standardized procedures are used to:

- Identify resource requirements,
- Order and acquire resources, and
- Mobilize resources.

The purpose of tracking and reporting is accountability. Resource accountability helps ensure responder safety and effective use of incident resources. As incident objectives are reached, resources may no longer be necessary. At this point, the recovery and demobilization process begins.

Recovery may involve the rehabilitation, replenishment, disposal, or retrograding of resources, while demobilization is the orderly, safe, and efficient return of an incident resource to its original location and status. And finally, any agreed-upon reimbursement is made.

When disaster strikes, we must be able to take full advantage of all available and qualified resources.

Standardized Approach to Resource Management

In this course you will learn how NIMS establishes a standardized approach for managing resources before, during, and after an incident. This standardized approach is based on the following underlying concepts:

- Consistency
- Standardization
- Coordination
- Use
- Information Management
- Credentialing

Consistency: Resource management provides a **consistent** method for identifying, acquiring, allocating, and tracking resources.

Standardization: Resource management includes **standardized** systems for classifying resources to improve the effectiveness of mutual aid agreements and assistance agreements.

Coordination: Resource management includes **coordination** to facilitate the integration of resources for optimal benefit.

Use: Resource management planning efforts incorporate **use** of all available resources from all levels of government, nongovernmental organizations, and the private sector, where appropriate.

Information Management: Resource management integrates **communications and information management** elements into its organizations, processes, technologies, and decision support.

Credentialing: Resource management includes the use of **credentialing** criteria that ensure consistent training, licensure, and certification standards.

Lesson 2:

Resource Management Planning

Resource Management Planning Process Overview

This lesson is organized around the following planning steps:

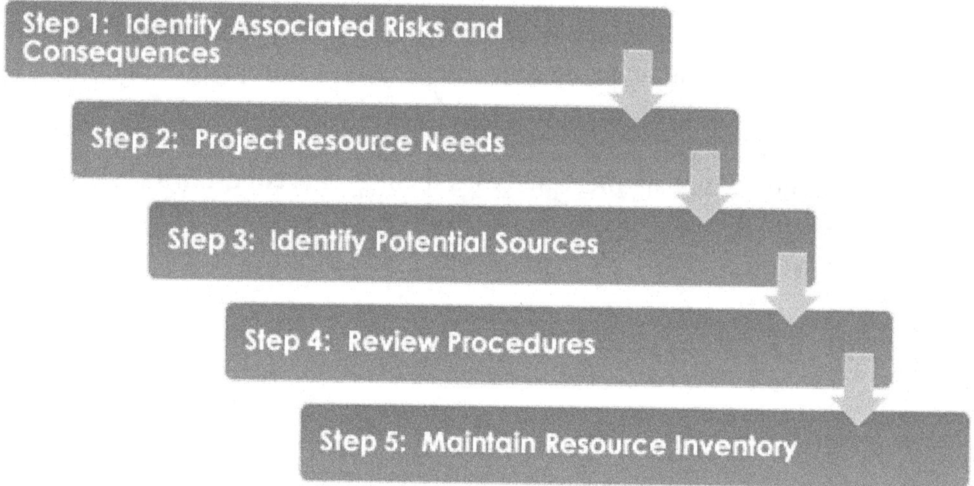

Risk-Based Planning

The planning process should include identifying resource needs based on the threats to and vulnerabilities of the jurisdiction and developing alternative strategies to obtain the needed resources. There are a number of methodologies that can be used for identifying your risks, but all methodologies should:

- Identify possible kinds of incidents and their related threats, risks, or consequences. (What might happen?)
- Quantify the likelihood of an occurrence of any given incidents. (How likely is it to happen?)
- Assess the most likely magnitude of any given incident. (How bad is it likely to be?)
- Assess the percent of the population at risk from any given incident. (How many people might be injured or killed?)
- Assess the severity of impact or likely consequences of any given incident. (How much damage is there likely to be?)

This analysis will result in a picture of the most likely incidents, their potential consequences, and needed resources.

Step 1: Identify Associated Risks and Consequences

The first step in establishing resource needs is to consider the related risks, including threats and consequences that your jurisdiction may face.

In identifying risks, it is important to consider the cascading events or related emergencies that may follow an incident. For example, an earthquake may cause:

- Building and bridge collapses.
- Hazardous materials spills.
- Utility outages.

Your jurisdiction's Emergency Operations Plan should include hazard analysis information.

Step 2: Project Resource Needs

After analyzing the risks, next determine what resources are needed to manage incidents. Some resources will be specific to only one risk or consequence; others may be useful for multiple risks or consequences.

Example: Urban rescue resources would likely only be needed for building collapses following a hurricane, but resources associated with traffic control would be needed to assist with debris removal, security, and damage to bridges and roads.

Researching Incidents

Reviewing case histories or interviewing managers of similar incidents can be helpful in researching infrequent or unfamiliar incidents. Sometimes needed resources are not immediately apparent.

For example, emergency managers in Oklahoma City had not considered the need to dispose of large quantities of biohazardous waste prior to the bombing of the Alfred P. Murrah Building.

Another frequently overlooked or underestimated category is the needs associated with ethnic groups, such as special dietary requirements.

Common Resources

Resources you identify fall into seven general groupings:

- Personnel: Includes Incident Command System "overhead" or management staff, technical specialists, Emergency Operations Center staff, operations staff, etc.
- Facilities: Includes office space, shelters, warehouses, etc.
- Equipment: Refers to pieces of equipment, with or without the personnel needed to operate them.
- Vehicles: Includes automobiles, buses, etc.
- Teams: Refers to groups of specially trained and equipped personnel, including needed equipment and supplies.
- Aircraft: Includes surveillance platforms, medevac, or cargo configurations.
- Supplies: Can span an enormous range from potable water to plywood. It is impossible to develop and maintain complete lists. A more efficient way to plan is to develop and maintain a current list of suppliers with comprehensive inventories.

Resource Typing

Thinking ahead about the appropriate configuration and capabilities of emergency resources can ensure that incidents receive the right resource for the job.

Resource typing enhances emergency preparedness, response, and recovery at all levels of government. Using consistent resource typing definitions helps the Incident Command request and deploy needed resources. Typing enables emergency management personnel to identify, locate, request, order, and track outside resources quickly and effectively.

The next lesson presents additional information on resource typing.

Benefits

The benefits of typed resource definitions include the improved ability of:

- Incident Commanders to make their resource requests.
- Emergency responders to know the capabilities of resources they are using.
- Resource managers in the Multiagency Coordination (MAC) System and/or Emergency Operations Centers (EOCs) to locate, mobilize, and track resources.

NIMS Requirements

To support State, territorial, tribal, and local governments in their resource typing efforts, the FEMA National Preparedness Directorate has coordinated the development, vetting, and publication of resource typing definitions. Jurisdictions should compare their resources to the NIMS resource typing definitions. Tier I response assets should be reported for incorporation into the national resource inventory. Jurisdictions are encouraged to inventory and type Tier II resources as well.

Step 3: Identify Potential Sources

Resources come from a variety of sources, including:

- Within your agency or jurisdiction.
- Mutual aid and assistance.
- Other levels of government.
- Volunteer organizations.
- Private-sector sources.
- Donations.

Agency or Jurisdiction Resources

The first source to consider is the current capability and inventory of your own agency or jurisdiction. During an incident, you must exhaust your own resources before you approach the next level of government for assistance. Consider:

- What kinds and types of resources are already owned by your agency, and are they suitable for use in emergencies?
- What kinds of supplies does your agency usually warehouse?
- What training and experience do agency personnel have?

Analysis of personnel should include not only their job-related training, skills, and experience, but additional experience, hobbies, or part-time job skills that might be useful. Keep in mind that outside-the-job experience can be both an asset and a liability.

Mutual Aid and Assistance

Mutual aid agreements and assistance agreements are agreements between agencies, organizations, and jurisdictions that provide a mechanism to quickly obtain emergency assistance in the form of personnel, equipment, materials, and other associated services.

The primary objective is to facilitate rapid, short-term deployment of emergency support prior to, during, and after an incident. A signed agreement does not obligate the provision or receipt of aid, but rather provides a tool for use should the incident dictate a need.

What Are Mutual Aid Agreements and Assistance Agreements?

Mutual aid agreements and assistance agreements are agreements between agencies, organizations, and jurisdictions that provide a mechanism to quickly obtain emergency assistance in the form of personnel, equipment, materials, and other associated services. The primary objective is to facilitate rapid, short-term deployment of emergency support prior to, during, and after an incident. A signed agreement does not obligate the provision or receipt of aid, but rather provides a tool for use should the incident dictate a need.

What Are the Different Types of Agreements?

There are several types of these kinds of agreements, including but not limited to the following:

- **Automatic Mutual Aid:** Agreements that permit the automatic dispatch and response of requested resources without incident-specific approvals. These agreements are usually basic contracts; some may be informal accords.
- **Local Mutual Aid:** Agreements between neighboring jurisdictions or organizations that involve a formal request for assistance and generally cover a larger geographic area than automatic mutual aid.
- **Regional Mutual Aid:** Substate regional mutual aid agreements between multiple jurisdictions that are often sponsored by a council of governments or a similar regional body.
- **Statewide/Intrastate Mutual Aid:** Agreements, often coordinated through the State, that incorporate both State and local governmental and nongovernmental resources in an attempt to increase preparedness statewide.
- **Interstate Agreements:** Out-of-State assistance through the Emergency Management Assistance Compact (EMAC) or other formal State-to-State agreements that support the response effort.
- **International Agreements:** Agreements between the United States and other nations for the exchange of Federal assets in an emergency.
- **Other Agreements:** Any agreement, whether formal or informal, used to request or provide assistance and/or resources among jurisdictions at any level of government (including foreign), nongovernmental organizations (NGOs), or the private sector.

Jurisdictions should be party to agreements with the appropriate jurisdictions and/or organizations (including NGOs and the private sector, where appropriate) from which they expect to receive, or to which they expect to provide, assistance. States should participate in interstate compacts and look to establish intrastate agreements that encompass all local jurisdictions. Authorized officials from each of the participating jurisdictions and/or organizations should collectively approve all mutual aid agreements and assistance agreements.

Memorandums of understanding and memorandums of agreement are needed with the private sector and NGOs, including community-based, faith-based, and national organizations such as the American Red Cross and the Salvation Army, to facilitate the timely delivery of assistance during incidents.

What Is Included in Agreements?

Agreements, preferably written, should include the following elements or provisions:

- Definitions of key terms used in the agreement
- Roles and responsibilities of individual parties
- Procedures for requesting and providing assistance
- Procedures, authorities, and rules for payment, reimbursement, and allocation of costs
- Notification procedures
- Protocols for interoperable communications
- Relationships with other agreements among jurisdictions
- Workers' compensation
- Treatment of liability and immunity
- Recognition of qualifications, licensure, and certifications
- Sharing agreements, as required
- Termination clause

Use of Agreements

Preincident agreements among all parties providing or requesting resources are necessary to enable effective and efficient resource management during incident operations.

Formal preincident agreements are established between parties (both governmental and nongovernmental) that might provide or request resources during incidents. These agreements ensure the efficient deployment of standardized, interoperable equipment and other incident resources during incident operations.

One example of a formal preincident agreement between States is the Emergency Management Assistance Compact (EMAC).

Lessons Learned: Mutual Aid and Assistance Agreements

Local Emergency Manager
We have negotiated mutual aid agreements with adjacent law enforcement, fire, public works, and EMS agencies. This expands our resource pool and also provides agreed-upon procedures for dispatch, resource management, and reimbursement. We are a pretty large jurisdiction for this State, but even so, we would not be able to manage a major disaster without help.

State Emergency Manager
Once our own State and local resources have been expended, our next best source of resources is through our EMAC agreements with the States adjacent to us. These resources are familiar, and able to respond in a relatively short time. The States also have clear procedures for dispatching them, managing them at the incident, and reimbursement. This ensures that no time is lost if we need assistance or to send resources to a neighboring jurisdiction.

Other Levels of Government

Public-sector emergency managers should have a good idea of resources available at all levels of government, their capabilities and support needs, and response times. Availability is not guaranteed. Members of the National Guard and military reserve units may not be available as incident resources if they have been deployed elsewhere.

You should assume that resources outside the incident area (State and Federal resources) will take up to 72 hours to arrive. It should also be reinforced that all resource requests to other levels of government must follow the established request procedures.

Volunteer Organizations

Many volunteer nongovernmental organizations (NGOs) play major roles in emergency response. Commonly referred to as Volunteer Organizations Active in Disasters, or VOAD, the number and degree of formal organizations vary from State to State.

Knowing what volunteer agencies are active in your area, what resources they can provide, and how to effectively activate and incorporate these resources is critical to your resource analysis process. It is helpful to include these organizations in your planning process.

Some jurisdictions have VOAD Councils designed to coordinate with each other and with public-sector entities. Such councils can be an extremely useful tool in both the planning and the activation processes, especially if resource requests can be forwarded to the council for resolution.

Involving Voluntary Agencies

Failure to include voluntary organizations in your planning and exercises will result in duplication of effort and/or resource shortfalls. Many will show up as "spontaneous volunteer organizations" and will not check in with either the Incident Commander or the Emergency Operations Center. This will result in:

- Failure to integrate VOAD resources into formal response, leading to loss of accountability.
- Potential safety issues.
- Public relations problems.
- Lack of confidence in the jurisdiction's entire emergency management ability to respond to an incident.

Lessons Learned: Unsolicited Donations

No single jurisdiction has the resources necessary to respond to a catastrophic disaster. Mutual aid resources are a primary asset during a major emergency, and most jurisdictions have formal mutual aid agreements that support their needs. Private-sector and donor assistance may be less well incorporated into the system, and without careful planning, may prove to be a liability rather than an asset.

The City of Santa Cruz, CA has experienced the hazards of not planning for unsolicited donations. One time, a boat loaded with supplies donated to Santa Cruz arrived along the coast, but Santa Cruz has no port facilities to offload. On another occasion, Santa Cruz received a tractor trailer loaded with tennis shoes... but only for the left foot!

Private-Sector Partners

Private-sector organizations play a key role before, during, and after an incident. First, they must provide for the welfare and protection of their employees in the workplace. In addition, emergency managers must work seamlessly with businesses that provide water, power, communication networks, transportation, medical care, security, and numerous other services upon which both response and recovery are particularly dependent.

During an incident, key private-sector partners should be involved in the local crisis decisionmaking process, or at least have a direct link to key local emergency managers. Communities cannot effectively respond to or recover from incidents without strong cooperative relations with the private sector.

Participation of the private sector varies based on the nature of the organization and the nature of the incident. The five distinct roles that private-sector organizations play are summarized in the table below:

Private-Sector Response Roles

Category	Role in This Category
Impacted Organization or Infrastructure	Private-sector organizations may be impacted by direct or indirect consequences of the incident. These include privately owned critical infrastructure, key resources, and other private-sector entities that are significant to local, regional, and national economic recovery from the incident. Examples of privately owned infrastructure include transportation, telecommunications, private utilities, financial institutions, and hospitals. Critical infrastructure and key resources (CIKR) are grouped into 18 sectors that together provide essential functions and services supporting various aspects of the American government, economy, and society.
Regulated and/or Responsible Party	Owners/operators of certain regulated facilities or hazardous operations may be legally responsible for preparing for and preventing incidents from occurring and responding to an incident once it occurs. For example, Federal regulations require owners/operators of nuclear power plants to maintain emergency plans and facilities and to perform assessments, prompt notifications, and training for a response to an incident.
Response Resource	Private-sector entities provide response resources (donated or compensated) during an incident – including specialized teams, essential service providers, equipment, and advanced technologies – through local public-private emergency plans or mutual aid and assistance agreements, or in response to requests from government and nongovernmental-volunteer initiatives.
Partner With State/Local Emergency Organizations	Private-sector entities may serve as partners in local and State emergency preparedness and response organizations and activities.

Components of the Nation's Economy	As the key element of the national economy, private-sector resilience and continuity of operations planning, as well as recovery and restoration from an actual incident, represent essential homeland security activities.

Private-Sector Responsibilities

Essential private-sector responsibilities include:

- Planning for the protection of employees, infrastructure, and facilities.
- Planning for the protection of information and the continuity of business operations.
- Planning for responding to and recovering from incidents that impact their own infrastructure and facilities.
- Collaborating with emergency management personnel before an incident occurs to ascertain what assistance may be necessary and how they can help.
- Developing and exercising emergency plans before an incident occurs.
- Where appropriate, establishing mutual aid agreements and assistance agreements to provide specific response capabilities.
- Providing assistance (including volunteers) to support local emergency management and public awareness during response and throughout the recovery process.

Donations

During incidents, private-sector sources frequently wish to contribute goods and services free or at a reduced cost. We will discuss unsolicited donations later in this course.

However, it is also important to have a procedure in place that clearly defines and documents the conditions under which goods and services are being offered. It is not unusual for jurisdictions to be billed at a later date for resources that were offered "free" in the initial response to the emergency. Making certain that the circumstances are clear helps ensure that donors are recognized for being good neighbors, and that there are no misunderstandings later.

Step 4: Review Procedures

Procedures and protocols should detail the specific actions to implement a plan or system. All emergency management/response personnel and their affiliated organizations should develop procedures and protocols that translate into specific, action-oriented checklists for use during incident response operations.

You may want to make sure that your procedures address the following resource management questions:

- How do you get that resource in the middle of the night on a weekend when the owner/supervisor is out of town?
- Do you have access to the necessary phone numbers and addresses?
- Will you have to pay for this resource? If so, what is the rate? Are there additional costs associated with emergency use or after-hours activation?
- Is purchasing authority delegated to the appropriate personnel in sufficient amounts to meet emergency needs?
- What emergency declarations or legal frameworks must be activated or invoked?
- How will the resource gain access to the incident scene?

Systems and Protocols

Effective resource management includes:

- **Systems:** Management information systems collect, update, and process resource data and track the status and location of resources.

  It is critical to have redundant information systems or backup systems to manage resources in the event that the primary system is disrupted or unavailable.
- **Protocols:** Preparedness organizations develop standard protocols to request resources, prioritize requests, activate and mobilize resources to incidents, and return resources to normal status.

Acquisition Strategies

Effective resource management includes establishing resource acquisition procedures. It is important to consider the tradeoffs (e.g., shelf life, warehousing costs) and determine the optimal acquisition strategies, including:

- Acquiring critical resources in advance and storing them in a warehouse (i.e., "stockpiling").

- Supplying resources "just in time," typically using a preincident contract.

Planning and resource accounting procedures should accommodate both types of resource supply.

Shelf-Life or Special Maintenance Considerations

An important part of the process is managing inventories with shelf-life or special maintenance considerations. Strict reliance on stockpiling raises issues concerning shelf life and durability; however, strict reliance on "just in time" resources raises its own concerns related to timely delivery.

Assets that are counted on for "just in time" need to be accurately accounted for to ensure that multiple jurisdictions or private-sector organizations are not relying solely on the same response asset, which can lead to shortages during a response. Those with resource management responsibilities should build sufficient funding into their budgets for periodic replenishment, preventive maintenance, and capital improvements. An integral part of acquisition procedures is developing methods and protocols for the handling and distribution of donated resources.

Purchase Authority

Most jurisdictions limit purchasing authority to specific people and specific limits. While administrative rules addressing financial issues may work fine in the 40-hour/daylight-only workweek, it may not serve the organization well in an off-hour emergency. Stories abound of responders forced to purchase supplies with personal credit cards because official fiscal support was not available. Each organization must:

- Determine who, at what level in the organization, has what amount of purchasing authority.
- Ensure that appropriate financial controls are observed at all levels.
- Ensure that appropriate training and refresher training on jurisdiction purchasing and documentation procedures is completed.

Controlling Access to the Scene

Planning efforts must consider the issues related to incident scene access. Convergence and self-dispatching represent a significant threat to scene safety and resource management. Your plans should include:

- A method for identifying authorized personnel from other jurisdictions, volunteer organizations, or commercial vendors.
- Procedures for clearing the incident scene of spectators, unauthorized volunteers, and survivors.
- Methods for securing the cleared scene and limiting access points.

Personnel qualifications and certification will be discussed in the Resource Typing lesson.

Perform a Legal Review of Procedures

You may want to have your legal counsel review your organization's legal foundations for resource management as well as your resource management plan and/or annex to the Emergency Operations Plan. For example:

- Goods and services frequently make a major leap in price following an incident. Many jurisdictions have put in place ordinances to prevent price gouging.
- Contracting procedures, such as the amount of time contracts must be advertised, may need to be suspended following an incident.

Emergency purchasing authority may need to be delegated to Incident Commanders, department heads, Logistics Section Chiefs, or emergency managers.

Additional Legal Considerations

Additional legal questions to consider include:

- Under what circumstances (if any) can personal property be commandeered?
- Are liability measures in place to protect both your jurisdiction and volunteers and their organizations?
- Does your organization have an incident contingency fund? Who can access it, and under what conditions?
- Do you have sufficient intergovernmental agreements in place to provide and receive mutual aid?

Step 6: Maintain Resource Inventory

After you have determined what you need, where you can find it, and how to procure it, the information needs to be organized, made accessible to those who need it, and maintained. Most organizations develop their own versions of "the yellow pages," including the type of resource, its owner, location, and procurement procedures.

Accessibility is also an issue. The most detailed inventory in the world is useless if staff can't access it. Inventories should be available in different formats stored at different locations. If the primary inventory is electronic, it may be advisable to have paper copies available for key Logistics and Finance/Administration workers, dispatchers, and Multiagency Coordination (MAC) System staff.

Keeping Information Up to Date

Maintaining such resource inventories is time-consuming work. It takes time and attention to detail to make sure all information is up to date, but there are few things more frustrating than discovering you do not have an after-hours contact for hardware stores when you need plywood at 3:00 in the morning.

Most organizations update on an annual or semiannual basis. There is software available that will e-mail your contacts and ask for updates automatically.

Planning for Interorganizational Issues

It is critically important to think through the relationships between and among the various command and coordination entities that are likely to be activated during an incident. Included in this analysis should be:

- ICS organization on incident.
- Dispatch organizations.
- Mutual aid cooperators.
- Unified Command.
- Area Command.
- Emergency service districts or other special mission governmental entities.
- Local, county, regional, and State EOCs.
- Multiagency Coordination (MAC) System entities such as MAC Groups, VOAD Councils, State Emergency Boards, etc.
- FEMA Regional Response Coordination Centers (RRCCs).
- Joint Field Offices (JFOs).
- Joint Information Centers (JICs).

A solution that works in one jurisdiction might be inappropriate (or illegal!) in another.

Dispatch centers or offices and agency ordering points manage resources on a day-to-day basis. Therefore, it is important to establish procedures that allow those who are unfamiliar with resource management procedures to integrate smoothly into these administrative structures during the stress and uncertainty inherent in an incident.

It is important that planners consider carefully the relationships among these structures as they relate to resource management.

Lesson 3: Resource Typing & Readiness

Resource Management: Preparedness Activities

It is essential for preparedness organizations to inventory and maintain current data on their available resources.

The inventory process involves:

- **Resource Typing:** Assigning a standardized typing designation to each resource that allows Incident Commanders to request and deploy resources.
- **Credentialing, Training, and Exercising:** Ensuring personnel are qualified, trained, and exercised to common standards that provide a foundation for the interoperability and compatibility of resources.

Introduction to Resource Typing

Emergencies occur throughout America every day. Emergency response involves a wide range of resources: people, equipment, and tools. But what resources are required to meet incident needs? How does the Incident Command know what to ask for? And how do resource managers know that they are fulfilling the request accurately?

The answer to all of these questions is by categorizing resources by capability and performance levels—**resource typing.**

Resource typing is a continuous process that facilitates accuracy in requesting and obtaining needed resources. Measurable definitions identifying the capabilities and performance levels for resources serve as the basis for resource typing.

Resource typing enhances emergency preparedness, response, and recovery by using consistent definitions that allow Incident Commanders to request and deploy the resources they need, and emergency management personnel to identify, locate, request, order, and track outside resources quickly and effectively.

Resource Typing Overview

Resource typing is the categorization, by capability, of the resources requested, deployed, and used in incidents. Measurable definitions identifying the capabilities and performance levels for resources serve as the basis for categories.

- Resource **kinds** may be divided into subcategories to define more precisely the resource capabilities needed to meet specific requirements.
- Resource **typing** is a continuous process designed to be as simple as possible to facilitate frequent use and accuracy in obtaining needed resources.

For example, a construction dump truck and a dump truck with a snow plow have different capabilities, capacities, and purposes. They would, therefore, be of different kinds and types.

The FEMA National Preparedness Directorate (NPD) has identified, promoted, and published resource typing definitions for the most commonly requested interstate resources. Resource typing definitions provide information to emergency managers and response personnel to ensure that they request and receive the appropriate resources.

NIMS encourages States, tribes, and local governments to take the necessary action to **inventory** and **type** Tier I response assets within the State that may be identified in the national inventory.

For example, resource typing definitions help ensure that generators used for pumping water are not confused with generators that provide electricity to buildings.

Tier I and Tier II Resources

FEMA NPD, in cooperation with all levels of government, tribes, nongovernmental organizations (NGOs), and private-sector entities, has developed the following levels of national resource typing definitions:

- **Tier I** represents resources that are included in the national resource typing definitions.
- **Tier II** includes all typed resources defined by the States, tribal and local jurisdictions, NGOs, and others that are not predefined in the Tier I definitions. (For example, local police usually are inventoried as Tier II resources.)

During the inventory process, States and tribes are encouraged to identify any resources that qualify as Tier I resources. Note that some States have expanded the national definitions to support intrastate and regional mutual aid agreements, assistance agreements, and compacts.

Tier I Criteria: National Resource Typing Definitions

At the national level, the NPD and its partners have developed criteria for Tier I resource typing definitions. These criteria may serve as a useful guide for States when developing their Tier II resource typing definitions.

States should inventory their assets to determine if Tier I resources are in the State. The NPD does not require States to report the number of resources—only that the States maintain an inventory in the event of an incident. States that do not have Tier I resources in their inventories are not required to purchase them.

Urban search and rescue task forces are an example of Tier I resources that must be inventoried for NIMS compliance.

Tier I Criteria for NIMS National Resource Typing Definitions

To meet the Tier I criteria for national resource typing definitions, the resource must:

1. Already exist as a defined, deployable interstate response resource for first responders.
2. Be exchanged and deployed with usage governed through interstate mutual aid agreements or compacts.
3. Be of sufficient capability to warrant being allocated and/or physically deployed nationally, if requested.
4. Have performance capability levels that can be identified as to **category, kind, and type.**
5. Be identified, inventoried, and tracked to determine availability status for response operations by the jurisdiction having authority.
6. Allow for command and control utilization under the NIMS Incident Command System (ICS).
7. Be sufficiently interoperable or compatible to allow for deployment through a defined system for resource ordering as authorized under interstate mutual aid agreements, compacts, and appropriate contracting mechanisms.

States and territories wishing to submit their Tier II resource typing definitions for consideration to be added to the Tier I national resource typing definitions need to:

1. E-mail the NPD at: FEMA-NIMS@dhs.gov.
2. Have an accompanying narrative that sufficiently explains the justification for a modification to be made to the Tier I resources.

3. Include, where appropriate, the category, kind, and types, as well as any credentialing requirements related to personnel or teams.
4. Include an electronic document that addresses points one through seven under Part A (i.e., using the format found in Appendix B of the National Incident Management System document).
5. Provide point of contact information for the NPD.

Upon receipt of the above information, the NPD will:

1. Conduct an internal review to reach a decision or to determine if any further guidance is needed by the appropriate external subject-matter experts.
2. Issue a public notification (if the decision is to proceed) along with a period for public comments, followed by an additional review process and then formal issuance of any addition or modification to Tier I NIMS national resource typing definitions.

Source: NIMS

Tier II Resource Typing

State, local, and tribal governments should inventory their Type II resources. Inventorying Type II resources makes resource sharing under mutual aid agreements, assistance agreements, the Emergency Management Assistance Compact (EMAC), and other agreements more efficient.

Fork lifts are an example of Tier II resources.

Resource Typing Steps

Resources are categorized by type definition. Measurable definitions identifying the capabilities and performance levels of resources are the basis for each category. Emergency management and response personnel may apply these definitions to inventory their resources.

Resources may be classified by kind. Resource kinds are broad classes that characterize like resources. The NIMS resources include the following kinds:

- Teams
- Equipment
- Supplies
- Vehicles
- Aircraft

Identifying and Typing Resources

Resource typing categorizes, by **capability,** the resources sought and mobilized in incident response and management. Measurable definitions identifying the capabilities and performance levels of resources serve as the basis for categories. Resource users at all levels utilize these definitions to identify and inventory resources easily. Resource typing is a continual process designed to be as simple as possible to facilitate frequent use and accuracy in obtaining needed resources. To allow resources to be deployed and used on a national basis, the NPD is responsible for facilitating the development of national guidance for the typing of resources and ensuring that these typed resources reflect operational capabilities.

Type specifically defines the level of capability a resource has. Type may vary by power, size, or capacity. Therefore, assigning a Type 1 label to a resource implies that it has a greater level of capability than a Type 2 of the same resource. The National Resource Typing definitions are broken into four distinct types. In some cases, a resource may have less than or more than four types. The type assigned to a resource or a component is based on a minimum level of capability described by the identified metric(s) for that resource.

Resource typing ensures that the Incident Command requests, receives, and deploys the resources it needs. Typing also ensures that emergency management and response personnel have the correct definitions available to request and/or deploy the correct resources to the incident.

Category describes the function for which a resource would be most useful. The table below lists the categories used in the national resource typing protocol (as of June 2007).

Category	
<ul><li>Transportation</li><li>Communications</li><li>Public works and engineering</li><li>Firefighting</li><li>Information and planning</li><li>Law enforcement and security</li><li>Mass care</li><li>Resource management</li></ul>	<ul><li>Health and medical</li><li>Search and rescue</li><li>Hazardous materials response</li><li>Food and water</li><li>Energy</li><li>Public information</li><li>Animals and agricultural issues</li><li>Volunteers and donations</li></ul>

Kind refers to broad classes that characterize like resources, such as teams, equipment, supplies, vehicles, and aircraft.

Measures (definitions) are used based on the kind of resource being typed. The mission envisioned determines the specific measure selected. The measure must be useful in describing a resource's capability to support the mission. Measures should identify the capability and/or capacity.

Resources are also designated in terms of tiers. **Tier I** resources include those resources that could be requested for deployment to a national incident. **Tier II** resources include those resources that do not have the capability to be requested as national resources but that may be deployed to State, tribal, or local incidents.

Implementing Resource Typing

FEMA has developed specific resource typing requirements for State, tribal, and local governments. These requirements include:

- Creating, updating, and maintaining an inventory of their resources in accordance with the NIMS resource typing definitions. DHS Homeland Security preparedness grant funds may be available for this purpose.
- Matching their resources/teams with the typing definitions.

Additionally, the State, tribal, or local agency conducting the inventory will make the determination that a specific resource meets the resource typing requirements and certify the resource as necessary.

Resources Not Matching Typing Definitions

If your resources do not match the NIMS resource typing definitions, you have two options:

- Work with your mutual aid and assistance agreement partners, State counterparts, etc. to inventory and type your resources within a Type II definition.
- Create and inventory all resources for local use only. Include these resources in the Resource Management Annex of your Emergency Operations Plan (EOP).

Do **not** try to force your resources into the NIMS resource typing definitions if they clearly don't fit. States and tribes should **not** purchase new resources to comply with the NIMS resource typing definitions.

NIMS Typing Definitions

As described previously, the NPD is working with discipline-specific working groups to develop typing definitions that serve as the standard for Tier I resources across the country.

The development of typed resources supports the establishment of:

- Comprehensive, national mutual aid and assistance agreements.
- Resource management and tracking systems.

Developing Typing Definitions

Through resource typing, disciplines examine their resources and identify the capabilities of a resource's components (teams, equipment). Because resource typing provides information about resource capabilities, emergency managers and others know the capability required for a requested resource to respond efficiently and effectively.

For some resources, the NPD working groups had typing definitions to use as a starting point. In other cases, no typing definitions existed. In these cases, the experts on each working group examined common types of resources and developed definitions by category and capability.

Typing definitions include all of the information needed for State, tribal, and local jurisdictions to determine whether their resources meet the minimum capabilities for each typing level.

Typing Definition Example

Resource: Hydraulic Excavator (Compact–Short Radius 1.75 cy to 0.61 cy Buckets)
Category: ESF #3: Public Works and Engineering
Kind: Equipment

	Type I	Type II	Type III	Type IV	Other
Manufacturer	**Model**	**Model**	**Model**	**Model**	**Model**
Bobcat	442		430		
Hitachi			ZX27U		
John Deere				27C ZTS	
Kobelco	245SRLC, 200SRLC, 135SRLC, ED150,	50SR-3, 35SR-3, 30SR-3	27SR-3	13SR	

	115SRDZ, 70SR				
New Holland	E80	E50.2SR, E30.2SR, E27.2SR			

Information Management Systems

Information Management Systems are used to:

- Collect, update, and process data;
- Track resources; and
- Display their readiness status.

These tools enhance information flow and provide real-time data in a fast-paced environment where different jurisdictions and functional agencies are managing different aspects of the incident life cycle and must coordinate their efforts. Examples include:

- Geographical information systems (GISs).
- Resource tracking systems.
- Transportation tracking systems.
- Inventory management systems.
- Reporting systems.

Equipment Preparedness

A critical component of preparedness is to:

- Acquire equipment that will perform to certain standards (as designated by organizations such as the National Fire Protection Association or National Institute of Standards and Technology), including the capability to be interoperable with equipment used by other jurisdictions or participating organizations.
- The development of a common understanding of the abilities of distinct types of equipment, to allow for better planning before an incident and rapid scaling and flexibility in meeting the needs of an incident.

Lessons Learned: Resource Management

In 1991 the City of Oakland, California, suffered a major conflagration in which hundreds of homes were lost and millions of dollars in damages were incurred. A major contributor to the problem was equipment incompatibility. The City of Oakland had water hydrant connections that did not meet the national standard. While the City had a special dispensation to use 2" rather than 2.5" connections, the difference meant that some mutual aid fire engines did not carry adaptors and could not access the city water supply. When the fire began, close-in, mutual aid engines that had adaptors were quickly depleted, and the City of Oakland did not have enough additional adaptors to equip the number of engines that responded from outside the immediate mutual aid area. This is an extreme example of the need for a standardized approach to emergency resource management. One of the primary goals of the National Incident Management System is to identify and establish the essential concepts and principles of resource management that will be covered in this course.

Interoperability

Interoperability ensures that resources can be moved and assigned across jurisdictional boundaries. No jurisdiction has all of the resources that could conceivably be needed during a major incident. Interoperable resources expand the resource pool and ensure an effective response.

Strategies to ensure interoperability include:

- Where national standards exist for connections, fittings, and hardware, these should be adopted by all jurisdictions.
- When possible, combine orders for standardized equipment.
- Where possible, make collective bulk orders to help ensure both best price and interoperability.

Interoperability Issues

Interoperability may be a major issue with communications equipment. While matching hardware may not be necessary in all cases, those who use 800 or 900 MHz systems may discover that their hardware is proprietary, making communication with others not on the system more difficult.

It is important to ensure that agencies share enough frequencies to provide communication during incidents. Many States have established statewide emergency frequencies that can be used for major mobilizations.

Another major issue with communications equipment is backup power and redundancy, as well as alternative communication methods for alert and warning systems.

IS-704 presents additional information on NIMS Communications and Information Management including interoperability.

Standard Operating Procedures

Consideration should be given to coordinating standard operating procedures (SOPs) where they might affect how a resource can be deployed.

For example, law enforcement agencies vary in restrictions on the use of arrest authorities and other procedures. Where possible, mutual aid and assistance partners should agree on such policies. When SOPs cannot be reconciled, it is important that mutual aid and assistance partners know the differences up front.

Testing Interoperability

Short of actual incident activation, the final test of all planning activities is to assess whether or not equipment and systems work under simulated conditions.

Testing equipment and systems should be incorporated into training and comprehensive exercises.

Personnel Qualifications and Certification

A critical element of NIMS preparedness is the use of national standards that allow for common or compatible structures for the qualification, licensure, and certification of emergency management and response personnel. Standards:

- Help ensure that these personnel possess the minimum knowledge, skills, and experience necessary to execute incident management and emergency response activities safely and effectively.
- Include training, experience, credentialing, validation, and physical and medical fitness.

Federal, State, tribal, and local certifying agencies, and professional and private organizations with personnel involved in emergency management and incident response,

are encouraged to credential those individuals in their respective disciplines or
jurisdictions.

Credentialing

The credentialing process involves an objective evaluation and documentation of an
individual's:

- Current certification, license, or degree;
- Training and experience; and
- Competence or proficiency.

Credentialing personnel ensures that they meet nationally accepted standards and are able
to perform specific tasks under specific conditions. Credentialing is separate from
badging, which takes place at the incident site in order to control access.

Credentialing Process

Scroll down to review the process, as recommended by the National Integration Center,
for credentialing under NIMS.

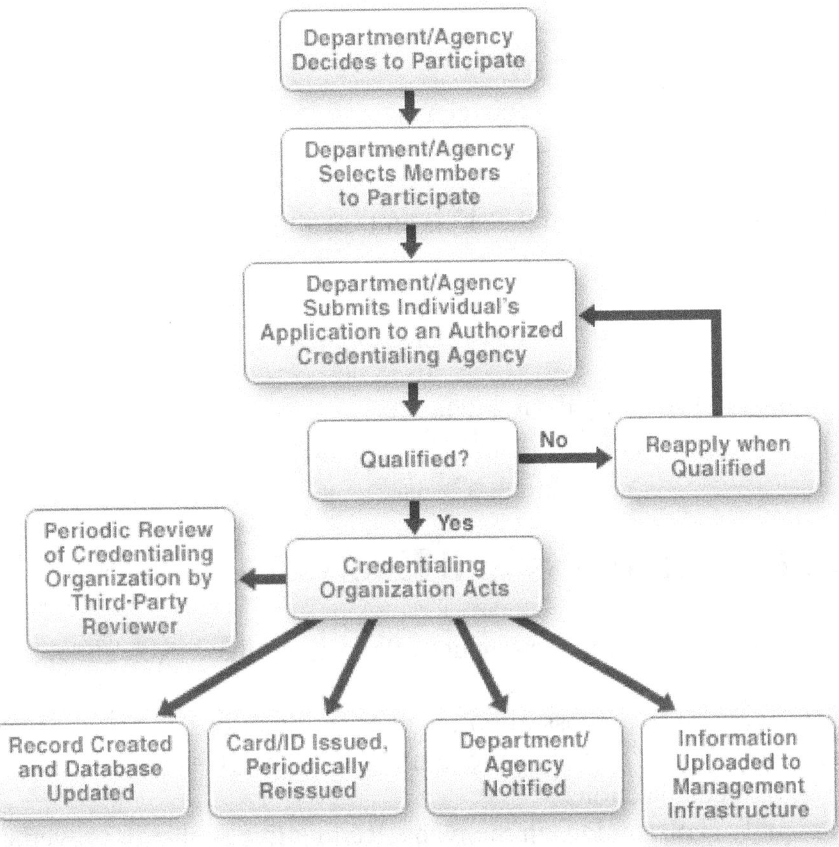

The process begins with the department/agency deciding to participate in the credentialing effort. Next the department/ agency selects members to participate in the credentialing effort.

The department/agency submits each individual's application to an authorized credentialing agency. That credentialing agency determines if the individual is qualified for the applied-for credential(s).

If the individual is found not qualified, he/she can reapply when qualified.

If the individual is found qualified, the credentialing agency acts as follows:

- Creates a record and updates the database.
- Issues a card/ID (and periodically reissues the card/ID as appropriate).
- Notifies the department/agency.
- Uploads the information to the management infrastructure.

The credentialing organization undergoes periodic review by a third-party reviewer.

Training

Personnel with roles in emergency management and incident response—including persons with leadership positions—should be trained to improve all-hazards capabilities.

The format for training depends on the skills and capabilities to be acquired and may include:

- Self-study or Web-based courses.
- Classroom sessions.
- Mentoring or shadowing during incidents.

Effective Preparedness and Exercises

Effective exercises are an essential element of the preparedness cycle. Exercises:

- Raise the general awareness of potential crisis situations.
- Ensure that key staff members are familiar with the plans and understand their roles and expected actions.
- Help identify shortcomings in the plans, leading to possible improvements.

Homeland Security Exercise and Evaluation Program

The DHS Homeland Security Exercise and Evaluation Program (HSEEP):

- Offers a common exercise policy.
- Provides program guidance that constitutes a national standard for exercises.
- Fosters consistent terminology that can be used by all exercise planners, regardless of the nature and composition of their sponsoring agency or organization.
- Provides useful tools that exercise managers can use to plan, conduct, and evaluate exercises to improve overall preparedness.

The next screens present a summary of key HSEEP concepts.

Types of Exercises

The exercise objectives provide a framework for scenario development, guide development of individual organizational objectives, and supply evaluation criteria. The objectives help you select from the following types of exercises:

- **Discussion-based exercises** familiarize participants with current plans, policies, agreements, and procedures, or may be used to develop new plans, policies, agreements, and procedures.
- **Operations-based exercises** validate plans, policies, agreements, and procedures; clarify roles and responsibilities; and identify resource gaps in an operational environment.

Discussion-Based Exercises

Discussion-based exercises include **seminars**, **workshops**, **tabletop exercises**, and **games**. These types of exercises are used:

- As a starting point in the building-block approach of escalating exercise complexity.
- To highlight existing plans, policies, interagency/interjurisdictional agreements, and procedures.
- As valuable tools for familiarizing agencies and personnel with current or expected capabilities of an entity.
- To focus on strategic, policy-oriented issues.

Seminars

Seminars involve bringing together those with a role or interest in the plan—Federal, State, tribal, local, private-sector, and nongovernmental emergency management and response personnel—to discuss the plan and initial concepts for an annual drill or more indepth comprehensive exercise.

The seminar does not involve an actual exercise of the plan. Instead, it is a meeting that enables each participant to become familiar with the plan and the roles, responsibilities, and procedures of those involved. A seminar can also be used to discuss and describe technical matters with involved, nontechnical personnel.

Workshops

Workshops differ from seminars in two important respects: participant interaction is increased, and the focus is on achieving or building a product (such as a draft plan or policy). Workshops are often used in conjunction with exercise development to determine objectives, develop scenarios, and define evaluation criteria. To be effective, workshops must be highly focused on a specific issue, and the desired outcome or goal must be clearly defined.

Tabletop Exercises

The tabletop exercise involves a meeting of Federal, State, tribal, local, private-sector, and nongovernmental emergency management officials and responders in a conference room or training setting. The format is usually informal with minimum stress involved. The exercise begins with the description of a simulated event and proceeds with discussions by the participants to evaluate the plan and response procedures and to resolve concerns regarding coordination and responsibilities.

Tabletop exercise participants are encouraged to discuss issues indepth and develop decisions through slow-paced problem solving, rather than the rapid, spontaneous decisionmaking that occurs under actual or simulated emergency conditions. Tabletop exercises are effective for evaluating group problem-solving, personnel contingencies, group message interpretation, information sharing, interagency coordination, and achievement of specific objectives.

Games

Games are a simulation of operations that often involve two or more teams and use rules, data, and procedures to depict an actual or assumed real-life situation. The goal of a game is to explore decisionmaking processes and the consequences of those decisions. A game differs from the tabletop in that the sequence of events affects, and is in turn affected by, decisions made by players.

Operations-Based Exercises

Operations-based exercises are:

- Used to validate the plans, policies, agreements, and procedures solidified in discussion-based exercises.
- Used to clarify roles and responsibilities, identify gaps in resources needed to implement plans and procedures, and improve individual and team performance.
- Characterized by actual reaction to simulated intelligence; response to emergency conditions; mobilization of apparatus, resources, and/or networks; and commitment of personnel, usually over an extended period of time.

Types of Operations-Based Exercises

Operations-based exercises include:

- Drills
- Functional Exercises
- Full-Scale Exercises

Drill

A drill is a low-level exercise that tests, develops, or maintains skills in a single incident response procedure. A drill:

- Is a coordinated, supervised activity usually used to validate a specific operation or function in a single agency or organization.
- May be part of a training program to provide instruction on new equipment, develop or validate new policies and procedures, or maintain current skills.
- Has a narrow focus but is conducted within a realistic environment.
- Provides instant feedback using established standards to measure performance.
- May be used to prepare personnel for larger scale exercises.

Functional Exercise

A functional exercise is the highest level exercise you can conduct without fully activating all aspects of your emergency action plan or evacuating residents. A functional exercise:

- Involves various levels of response agencies and emergency management personnel.
- Involves the simulation of a facility failure or other specified events that require rapid responses by trained personnel "acting out" their actual roles.
- Takes place in a stress-induced environment with time constraints.
- Evaluates both the internal capabilities and responses of all levels of responders and emergency management officials.
- Evaluates the coordination activities between all levels of responders and emergency management personnel.

Full-Scale Exercise

A full-scale exercise:

- Is an interactive exercise designed to evaluate the operational capability of all facets of the emergency management system under review in a highly realistic and stressful environment.
- Differs from a functional exercise by involving actual field movement and mobilization, instead of simulation.

The realism of the full-scale exercise can be conveyed through on-scene actions and decisions, simulated "disaster survivors," communication devices, equipment deployment, and resource and personnel allocation.

Planning Effective Exercises

Although the exercise types will vary significantly in terms of scope and scale, the same general framework can be applied when planning most of the exercise types.

When developing exercises, it is important to:

- Define the purpose of the exercise.
- Assemble the planning team.
- Develop the scenario.
- Develop exercise guidelines.
- Prepare exercise materials and evaluator guides.
- Complete post-exercise evaluation.

Define the Purpose of the Exercise

A clear definition of the need for the exercise and the purpose for conducting it will aid the planning process by clarifying who should be involved and exercise scope (e.g., tabletop, game, full-scale).

The following need and purpose statements were based on a tabletop exercise template provided by Alliant Energy: "Our business is highly dependent on moving information across telecommunication networks. We need to be prepared to continue important business activities even if telecommunication networks stop functioning. The purpose of this exercise is to ensure that business groups can adapt to unpracticed emergency situations, like loss of telecommunication networks, and understand the actions that may be needed to keep important business functions operating."

Assemble the Planning Team

The size of the planning team and representation on it is dependent on the scope of the exercise. The team should include representatives from all the major facility organizations involved in the exercise and local law enforcement and first responders.

Develop the Scenario

The planning team's initial task is development of the exercise scenario. The scenario should be a plausible event scaled to the purpose of the exercise.

The following sample scenario was developed for a full-scale exercise: "An individual wearing a backpack was found lying unconscious inside the north gate. The backpack was leaking an orange liquid. A security officer approached the individual and has been rendered unconscious. An unidentified individual was seen running from the vicinity of the administration building and has caused an explosion resulting in a fire inside the building. His current whereabouts are unknown but he is believed to be somewhere on the site."

Develop Exercise Guidelines

Depending on the type of exercise and the scenario, the planning team should describe any limitations placed on the design, development, and implementation of the exercise. Limitations could be the ability of responders to participate, lengthy authorization protocols, areas that may be off-limits for safety reasons, or financial constraints.

The following is an example of a guideline: "No personnel may enter the switchyard at any time because it will continue to be energized."

Prepare Exercise Materials and Evaluator Guides

Participants should receive invitation letters describing the exercise purpose and goal; scenario descriptions pertaining to their role; and safety, health, and logistics plans. Equally important are the guidelines developed for the observers who will be evaluating actions and decisions as the exercise unfolds.

Complete Post-Exercise Evaluation

Post-exercise evaluations provide the basis for improving the plans or procedures that were tested as part of the exercise.

Post-Exercise Evaluation

A post-exercise evaluation is completed following all exercises. Post-exercise evaluations include the following elements:

- Hot Wash
- Debrief
- After-Action Report (AAR)
- Improvement Plan

Hot Wash

A hot wash is a facilitated discussion held immediately following an exercise among exercise players from each functional area. It is designed to capture feedback about any issues, concerns, or proposed improvements players may have about the exercise. The hot wash is an opportunity for players to voice their opinions on the exercise and their own performance. This facilitated meeting allows players to participate in a self-assessment of the exercise play and provides a general assessment of how the jurisdiction performed in the exercise. At this time, evaluators can also seek clarification on certain actions and what prompted players to take them. Evaluators should take notes during the hot wash and include these observations in their analysis. The hot wash should last no more than 30 minutes.

Debrief

A debriefing is a forum for planners, facilitators, controllers, and evaluators to review and provide feedback after the exercise is held. It should be a facilitated discussion that allows each person an opportunity to provide an overview of the functional area they observed and document both strengths and areas for improvement. Debriefs should be facilitated by the exercise planning team leader or the exercise program manager; results should be captured for inclusion in the after-action report and improvement plan. A debriefing is different from a hot wash, in that a hot wash is intended for players to provide feedback.

After-Action Report

An after-action report (AAR) should be developed upon conclusion of the exercise. The purpose of an AAR is to provide feedback to participants on their performance during the exercise. The AAR summarizes exercise events and analyzes performance of the tasks identified as important during the planning process. It also evaluates achievement of the selected exercise objectives and demonstration of the overall capabilities. After the AAR is complete, the last step is to develop an improvement plan. Its purpose is to convert lessons learned from the exercise into concrete, measurable steps that result in improved response capabilities.

Improvement Plan

The last step is to develop an improvement plan to convert lessons learned from the exercise into concrete, measurable steps that result in improved response capabilities. The improvement plan lists the corrective actions that will be taken, the responsible party or agency, and the expected completion date. The improvement plan is incorporated into the final after-action report.

Summary: Continuum of Exercises

The diagram below summarizes the continuum of discussed-based to operations-based exercises presented in this lesson. As the level of capabilities exercised is increased, the commitment needed for planning and training time also increases.

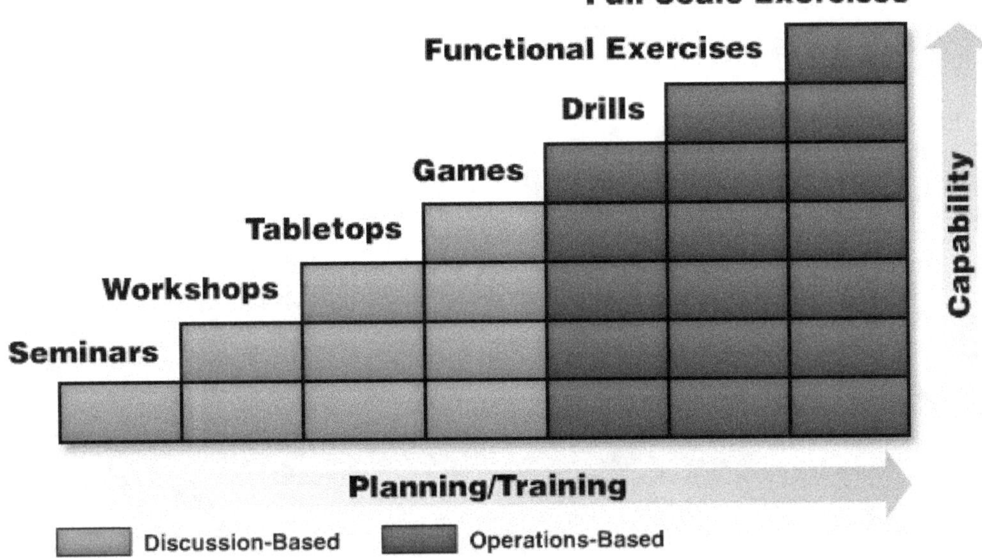

Full-Scale Exercises
Functional Exercises
Drills
Games
Tabletops
Workshops
Seminars
Capability
Planning/Training
Discussion-Based
Operations-Based

Lesson 4:

Resource Management During Incidents

Managing Resources: Overview

Following an incident, NIMS promotes the use of a standardized seven-step cycle for managing resources.

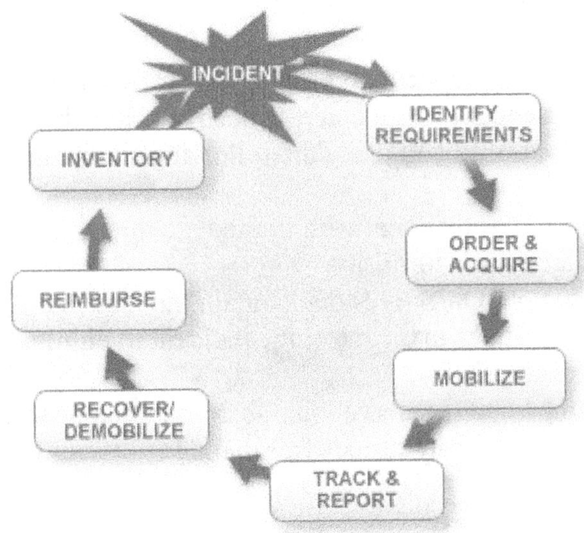

It is important to remember that resource management activities must occur on a continual basis to ensure that resources are ready for mobilization.

Step 1: Identify Requirements

When an incident occurs, personnel who have resource management responsibilities should continually identify, refine, and validate resource requirements. This process includes identifying:

- What and how much is needed.
- Where and when it is needed.
- Who will be receiving or using it.

Resource availability and requirements constantly change as the incident evolves. Coordination among all response partners should begin as early as possible, preferably prior to incident response activities.

Sizeup

The first step in determining resource needs is a thorough assessment or "sizeup" of the current incident situation and future incident potential.

This assessment provides the foundation for the incident objectives, and without it, it is impossible to identify the full range of resources that will be needed.

Establish Incident Objectives

The Incident Commander develops **incident objectives**—a statement of what is to be accomplished on the incident. Not all incident objectives have the same importance. Incident objectives can be prioritized using the following simple mnemonic:

- Life Safety: Objectives that deal with immediate threats to the safety of the public and responders are the first priority.
- Incident Stabilization: Objectives that contain the incident to keep it from expanding and objectives that control the incident to eliminate or mitigate the cause are the second priority.
- Property/Environmental Conservation: Objectives that deal with issues of protecting public and private property or damage to the environment are the third priority.

Lessons Learned: Establishing Incident Objectives

Incident objectives are not necessarily completed in sequence determined by priority. It may be necessary to complete an objective related to incident stabilization before a life safety objective can be completed. Using the LIP mnemonic helps prioritize incident objectives. This device can also be used to prioritize multiple incidents, with those incidents having significant life safety issues being given a higher priority than those with lesser or no life safety issues.

Incident Commander

Our assessment of the earthen dam determines that the water level must be lowered quickly in order to reduce the danger of the dam's collapse causing catastrophic flooding. One of my objectives is, "Reduce water level behind dam 3 feet by 0800 hours tomorrow." This is a well written objective because it is measurable. It will be clear if this objective has been completed, and will be easy to monitor to make sure the timeline is being met.

Incident Action Planning Process

The management by objectives focus of ICS is reinforced and implemented through the planning process. The Incident Action Planning (IAP) process steps include:

- Development of incident objectives and strategy.
- Development of tactics and resource assignments.
- Detailed incident and resource assessment, including safety concerns.
- Required logistical support.
- Consideration of public information and interagency issues.
- Documentation of assignments and required support on the written IAP.
- Monitored implementation.

Implementing the formal planning process early in the incident, and maintaining the discipline imposed by it, helps the ICS organization attain its objectives.

Strategies, Tactics, and Resources

The Operations Section Chief develops strategies and detailed tactics for accomplishing the incident objectives. By assigning resources to execute each tactic, the Operations Section Chief can identify resource needs.

The Operational Planning Worksheet (ICS Form 215) is used to indicate the kind and type of resources needed to implement the recommended tactics to meet the incident objectives. This worksheet includes the number of resources on site, ordered, and needed.

Operational Planning Worksheet

Below is the first part of the form. Note that each work assignment is described along with the types of resources required, number of resources at the scene, and total number of additional resources.

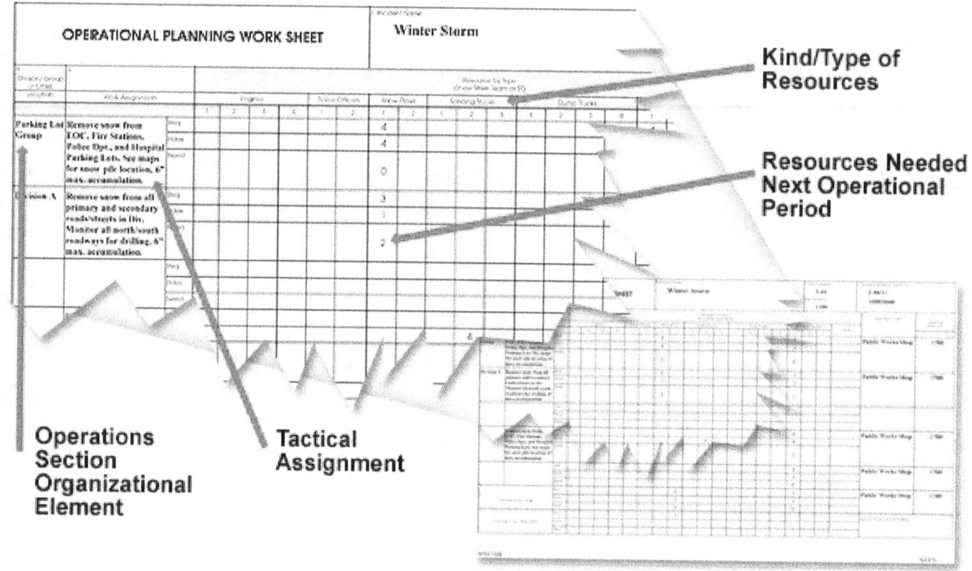

The other half of the form specifies where and when resources should arrive at the incident scene.

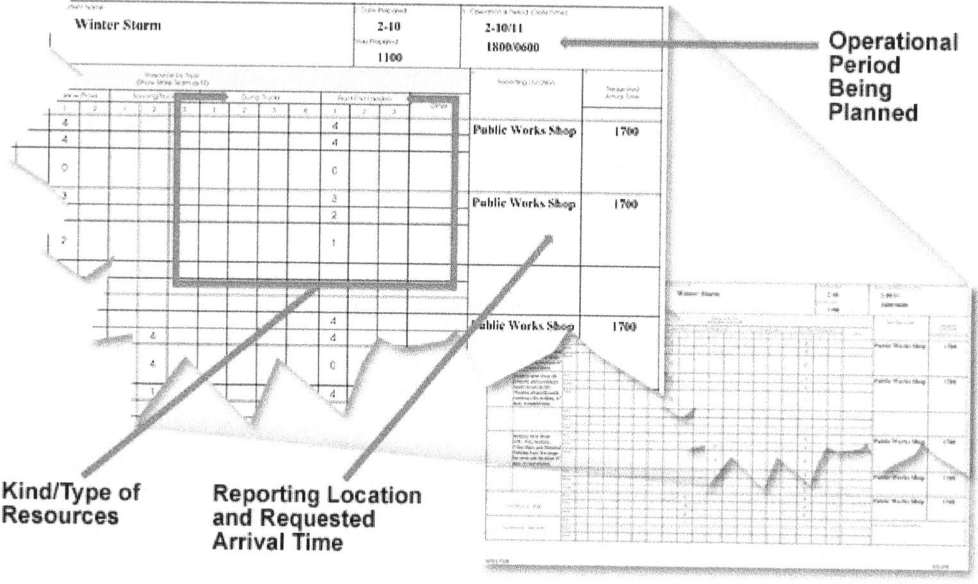

Supervisory and Support Resources

It is important that the incident organization's ability to supervise and support additional resources is in place prior to requesting them. As a consequence, more supervisory personnel may be needed to maintain adequate span of control, and support personnel may be added to ensure adequate planning and logistics.

Personnel and logistical support factors (e.g., equipping, transporting, feeding, providing medical care, etc.) must be considered in determining tactical operations. Lack of logistical support can mean the difference between success and failure.

Step 2: Order and Acquire

Standardized resource-ordering procedures are used when requests for resources cannot be fulfilled locally. Typically, these requests are forwarded first to an adjacent locality or substate region and then to the State.

Decisions about resource allocation are based on organization or agency protocol and possibly the resource demands of other incidents.

Mutual aid and assistance resources will be mobilized only with the consent of the jurisdiction that is being asked to provide the requested resources. Discrepancies between requested resources and those available for delivery must be communicated to the requestor.

Initial Commitment of Resources

Typically, incidents will have an initial commitment of resources assigned.

As incidents grow in size and/or complexity, more tactical resources may be required and the Incident Commander may augment existing resources with additional personnel and equipment.

Dispatch organizations service incidents on a first-come, first-served basis with the emergency response resources in the dispatch pool. Ordinarily, dispatchers have the authority to activate first-tier mutual aid and assistance resources.

Activating Formalized Resource-Ordering Protocols

More formalized resource-ordering protocols and the use of a Multiagency Coordination (MAC) Group or policy group may be required when:

- The organization does not have the authority to request resources beyond the local mutual aid and assistance agreements.
- The dispatch workload increases to the point where additional resources are needed to coordinate resource allocations.

- It is necessary to prioritize limited resources among incidents.

Resource Ordering Responsibilities: Overview

The chart below summarizes the resource ordering activities within the incident command organization:

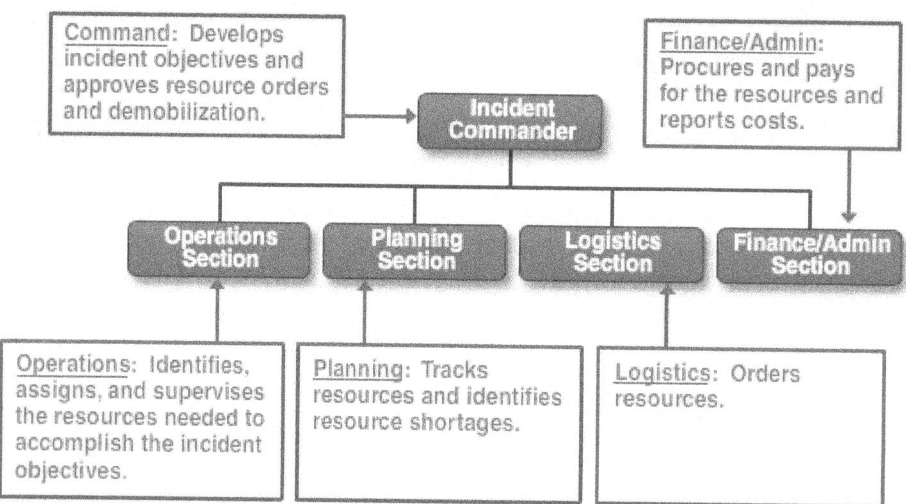

Avoid Bypassing Ordering Systems

Those responsible for managing resources, including public officials, should recognize that reaching around the official resource coordination process within the Multiagency Coordination System supporting the incident creates serious problems.

In other words, even if you think it is helpful, never send resources to the scene that have not been requested through the established system.

Requests from outside the established system for ordering resources can put responders at risk, and at best typically lead to inefficient use and/or lack of accounting of resources.

Establishing Resource Ordering Guidelines

The Incident Commander should communicate:

- **Who within the organization may place an order with Logistics.** This authority may be restricted to Section Chiefs and/or Command Staff, or may be delegated further down the chain of command.
- **What resource requests require the Incident Commander's approval.** The Incident Commander may want to review and approve any nonroutine requests, especially if they are expensive or require outside agency participation.
- **What resource requests may be ordered without the Incident Commander's approval.** It may not be efficient for the Incident Commander to review and approve all resource orders for routine supplies, food, etc., on a major incident.

Establishing Purchasing Guidelines

The Incident Commander should establish guidelines for emergency purchasing. Finance/Administration and Logistics staff must understand purchasing rules, especially if different rules apply during an emergency than day to day.

Writing these in a formal delegation of authority ensures that appropriate fiscal controls are in place, and that the Incident Management Team expends funds in accordance with the direction of the jurisdiction's agency administrator.

The Resource Order: Elements

The resource order is used to request personnel, tactical, and support resources. Even though different formats exist, every resource order should contain the following essential elements of information:

- Incident name
- Order and/or request number
- Date and time of order
- Quantity, kind, and type of resources needed (include special support needs as appropriate)
- Reporting location and contact (specific)
- Requested time of delivery (specific, not simply ASAP)
- Communications system to be used
- Person/title placing request
- Callback phone number for clarification or additional information
- For State and Federal agencies, a way to reference the originating office's order number

The Resource Order: Documentation

Resource orders should also document action taken on a request, including but not limited to:

- Contacts with sources or potential sources for the resource request.
- Source for the responding resource.
- Identification of the responding resource (name, ID number, transporting company, etc.).
- Estimated time of arrival.
- Estimated cost.
- Changes to the order made by Command, or the position placing the order.

Such detailed information is often critical in tracking resource status through multiple staff changes and operational periods.

Resource Order (ICS 308)

The Logistics Section may use the Resource Order form (ICS 308) to record the type and quantity of resources requested to be ordered. In addition, this form is used to track the status of the resources after they are received.

Request Number	Ordered Date/Time	From / To	QTY	RESOURCE REQUESTED	Needed Date/Time	Deliver To	To / From	Time	Agency ID	RESOURCE ASSIGNED	ETD / ETA	RELEASED Date	RELEASED To	Time / ETA
0-1	04/05 1000	10 M. Smith/ F. Able	1	Entomologist	04-07 1200	field action taken	T. Pole/ C. Davis	1030	PPQ 05	Bill Paxton	0800/ 1030			
0-2	04/05 1000	10 M. Smith/ F. Able	1	Entomologist	04-07 1200	field action taken	T. Pole/ C. Davis	1030	PPQ 05	Martha Hill	0800/ 1030			
0-3	04/06 1300	20 T. Fray/ F. Able	1	Operations S.C.	04-08 0800	ICP	T. Pole/ C. Davis	1310	PPQ 25	Brent Woods	4-7/ 1300 4-7 1900			

Tasking by Requirements

Occasionally, incident personnel may not know the specific resource or mix of resources necessary to complete a task. In such situations, it is advisable to state the requirement rather than request specific tactical or support resources. By clearly identifying the requirement, the agency fulfilling the order has the discretion to determine the optimal mix of resources and support needed.

For example, many local governments use a requirements-based approach with the American Red Cross for providing shelter services. The order describes the population needing shelter (location, size, special needs, and estimated timeframe) and the American Red Cross selects an appropriate facility and provides staff, equipment and supplies, and other resources.

Placing Orders

During smaller incidents, where only one jurisdiction or agency is primarily involved, the resource order is typically prepared at the incident, approved by the Incident Commander, and transmitted from the incident to the jurisdiction or agency ordering point. Methods for placing orders may include:

- Voice (by telephone or radio) or fax.
- Computer or digital display terminal.

For all incidents, using a single-point ordering system is the preferred approach.

Single-Point Resource Ordering: The concept of single-point resource ordering is that the burden of finding the requested resources is placed on the responsible jurisdiction/agency dispatch/ordering center and not on the incident organization.

Single-point resource ordering (i.e., ordering all resources through one dispatch/ordering center) is usually the preferred method.

However, single-point resource ordering may not be feasible when:

- The dispatch/ordering center becomes overloaded with other activity and is unable to handle new requests in a timely manner.
- Assisting agencies at the incident have policies that require all resource orders be made through their respective dispatch/ordering centers.
- Special situations relating to the order necessitate that personnel at the incident discuss the details of the request directly with an off-site agency or private-sector provider.

Multipoint Resource Ordering: Multipoint ordering is when the incident orders resources from several different ordering points and/or the private sector. **Multipoint off-incident resource ordering should be done only when necessary.**

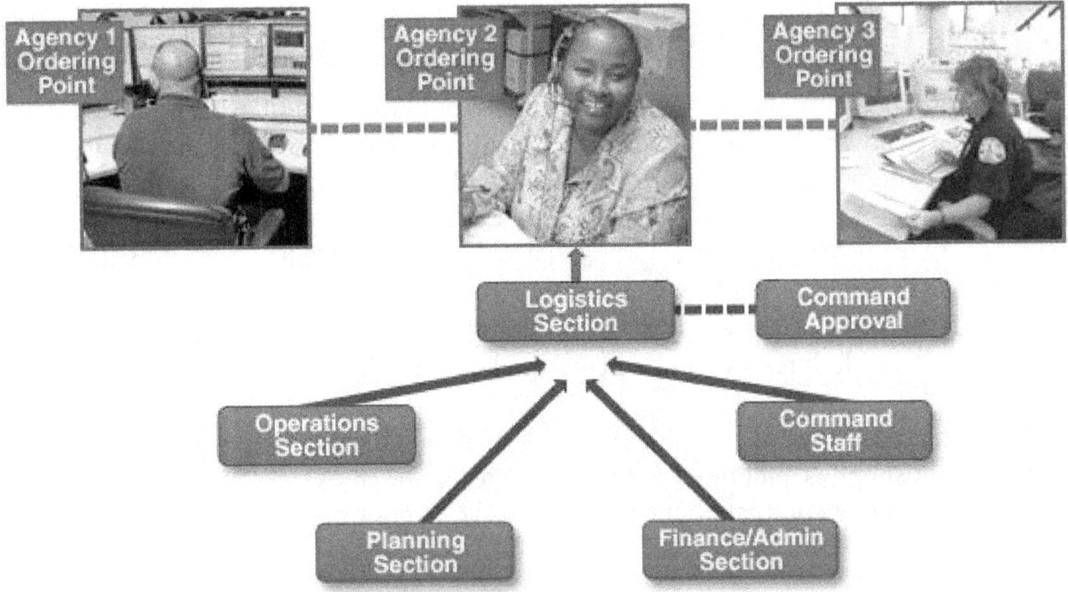

Multipoint ordering places a heavier load on incident personnel by requiring them to place orders through two or more ordering points. This method of ordering also requires tremendous coordination between and among ordering points, and increases the chances of lost or duplicated orders.

Step 3: Mobilize

Incident resources mobilize as soon as they are notified through established channels. Mobilization notifications should include:

- The date, time, and place of departure.
- Mode of transportation to the incident.
- Estimated date and time of arrival.
- Reporting location (address, contact name, and phone number).
- Anticipated incident assignment.
- Anticipated duration of deployment.
- Resource order number.
- Incident number.
- Applicable cost and funding codes.

When resources arrive on scene, they must be formally checked in.

Mobilization Procedures

Mobilization procedures should detail how staff should expect authorized notification, and designate who will physically perform the call-out. Procedures should also describe the agency's policy concerning self-dispatching and freelancing.

There are a number of software programs that can perform simultaneous alphanumeric notifications via pager, or deliver voice messages over the telephone. Backup procedures should be developed for incidents in which normal activation procedures could be disrupted by utility failures, such as an earthquake or hurricane.

Mobilization procedures must be augmented with detailed checklists, appropriate equipment and supplies, and other job aids such as phone trees or pyramid re-call lists so that activation can be completed quickly.

Step 4: Track and Report

Resource tracking is a standardized, integrated process conducted prior to, during, and after an incident to:

- Provide a clear picture of where resources are located.
- Help staff prepare to receive resources.
- Protect the safety and security of personnel, equipment, and supplies.
- Enable resource coordination and movement.

Resources are tracked using established procedures continuously from mobilization through demobilization.

Resource Tracking and Reporting Responsibilities

Resource tracking responsibilities are shared as follows:

- The **Planning Section** is responsible for tracking all resources assigned to the incident and their status (assigned, available, out of service).
- The **Operations Section** is responsible for tracking the movement of resources within the Operations Section itself.
- The **Finance/Administration Section** is responsible for ensuring the cost-effectiveness of resources.

ICS classifies tactical resources into one of three categories based on their status. These categories are:

- **Assigned** – Currently working on an assignment under the direction of a supervisor
- **Available** – Ready for immediate assignment and has been issued all required equipment
- **Out of Service** – Not available or ready to be assigned (e.g., maintenance issues, rest periods)

Accounting for Responders

As soon as the incident is discovered and reported, and often even before responders are dispatched, volunteers, survivors, and spectators will converge at the scene. When responders arrive, they must separate first spectators and then volunteers from disaster survivors, and secure a perimeter around the incident.

Securing a perimeter allows the incident response organization to:

- Establish resource accountability.
- Provide security and force protection.
- Ensure safety of responders and the public.

Establishing Access Procedures

It is important to have advanced procedures in place for:

- Establishing controlled points of access for authorized personnel.
- Distinguishing agency personnel who have been formally requested from those who self-dispatched.
- Verifying the identity, qualifications, and deployment authorization of personnel with special badges.
- Establishing affiliation access procedures to permit critical infrastructure owners and operators to send in repair crews and other personnel to expedite the restoration of their facilities and services.

Check-In Process

The Incident Command System uses a simple and effective resource check-in process to establish resource accountability at an incident.

The Planning Section Resources Unit establishes and conducts the check-in function at designated incident locations. If the Resources Unit has not been activated, the responsibility for ensuring check-in will be with the Incident Commander or Planning Section Chief. Formal resource check-in may be done on an ICS Form 211 Check-In List.

Check-In Process: Information Collected

Information collected at check-in is used for tracking, resource assignment, and financial purposes, and includes:

- Date and time of check-in.
- Name of resource.
- Home base.
- Departure point.
- Order number and resource filled.
- Resource Leader name and personnel manifest (if applicable).
- Other qualifications.
- Travel method.

Depending on agency policy, the Planning Section Resources Unit may contact the dispatch organization to confirm the arrival of resources, personnel may contact their agency ordering point to confirm their arrival, or the system may assume on-time arrival unless specifically notified otherwise.

Resource Status-Keeping Systems

There are many resource-tracking systems, ranging from simple status sheets to sophisticated computer-based systems. Regardless of the system used, it must:

- Account for the overall status of resources at the incident.
- Track movement of Operations personnel into and out of the incident "hot zone."
- Be able to handle day-to-day resource tracking, and also be flexible enough to track large numbers of multidisciplinary resources that may respond to a large, rapidly expanding incident.
- Have a backup mechanism in the event on-scene tracking breaks down.

The more hazardous the tactics being implemented on the incident, the more important it is to maintain accurate resource status information.

- **Manual Recordkeeping on Forms.** The following ICS forms can be used for resource tracking: the resources summary of the Incident Briefing (ICS Form 201), Check-In List (ICS Form 211), and Assignment List (ICS Form 204).
- **Card Systems.** Several versions are available that allow for maintaining status of resources on cards. One of these systems has different-colored T-shaped cards for each kind of resource. The cards are formatted to record various kinds of information about the resource. The cards are filed in racks by current location.
- **Magnetic Symbols on Maps or Status Boards.** Symbols can be prepared in different shapes, sizes, and colors with space to add a resource designator. The symbols are placed on maps or on boards indicating locations designated to match the incident.
- **Computer Systems.** A laptop computer can be used with a simple file management or spreadsheet program to maintain information on resources. These systems can be used to compile check-in information and then be maintained to reflect current resource status.

Best Practice: "Passport" System

The "Passport" system is an on-scene resource-tracking system that is in common use in fire departments across the country. The system includes three Velcro-backed name tags and a special helmet shield for each employee. When the employee reports for work, he or she places the name tags on three "passports." The primary passport is carried on the driver's-side door of the apparatus to which the employee is assigned. The secondary passport is carried on the passenger-side door, and the third is left at the fire station.

Upon arrival at an incident, the apparatus officer gives the primary passport to the Incident Commander, or the Division/Group Supervisor to which the resource is being assigned. The Incident Commander or Division/Group Supervisor will keep the passport until the resource is released from his or her supervision, when it will be returned to the company officer. The secondary passport may either remain with the apparatus, or be collected by the Resources Unit to aid overall incident resource tracking. The third passport serves as a backup mechanism documenting what personnel are on the apparatus that shift.

The helmet shield is placed on the employee's helmet upon receiving an incident assignment. The shield provides an easy visual indication of resource status and helps control freelancing.

Step 5: Recover/Demobilize

Recovery involves the final disposition of all resources, including those located at the incident site and at fixed facilities. During this process, resources are rehabilitated, replenished, disposed of, and/or retrograded.

Demobilization is the orderly, safe, and efficient return of an incident resource to its original location and status. Demobilization planning should begin as soon as possible to facilitate accountability of the resources. During demobilization, the Incident Command and Multiagency Coordination System elements coordinate to prioritize critical resource needs and reassign resources (if necessary).

Nonexpendable Resources

Nonexpendable resources (such as personnel, firetrucks, and durable equipment) are fully accounted for both during the incident and when they are returned to the providing organization. The organization then restores the resources to full functional capability and readies them for the next mobilization. Broken or lost items should be replaced through the appropriate resupply process, by the organization with invoicing responsibility for the incident, or as defined in existing agreements. It is critical that fixed-facility resources also be restored to their full functional capability in order to ensure readiness for the next mobilization. In the case of human resources, such as Incident Management Teams, adequate rest and recuperation time and facilities should be provided. Important occupational health and mental health issues should also be addressed, including monitoring the immediate and long-term effects of the incident (chronic and acute) on emergency management/response personnel.

Expendable Resources

Expendable resources (such as water, food, fuel, and other one-time-use supplies) must be fully accounted for. The incident management organization bears the costs of expendable resources, as authorized in financial agreements executed by preparedness organizations. Restocking occurs at the point from which a resource was issued. Returned resources that are not in restorable condition (whether expendable or nonexpendable) must be declared as excess according to established regulations and policies of the controlling jurisdiction, agency, or organization. Waste management is of special note in the process of recovering resources, as resources that require special handling and disposition (e.g., biological waste and contaminated supplies, debris, and equipment) are handled according to established regulations and policies.

Demobilization Responsibilities

Demobilization planning is informal and is executed by the Incident Commander, who follows agency protocols. However, on a complex incident, a formal demobilization plan and process should be followed. The chart below summarizes demobilization responsibilities on a complex incident.

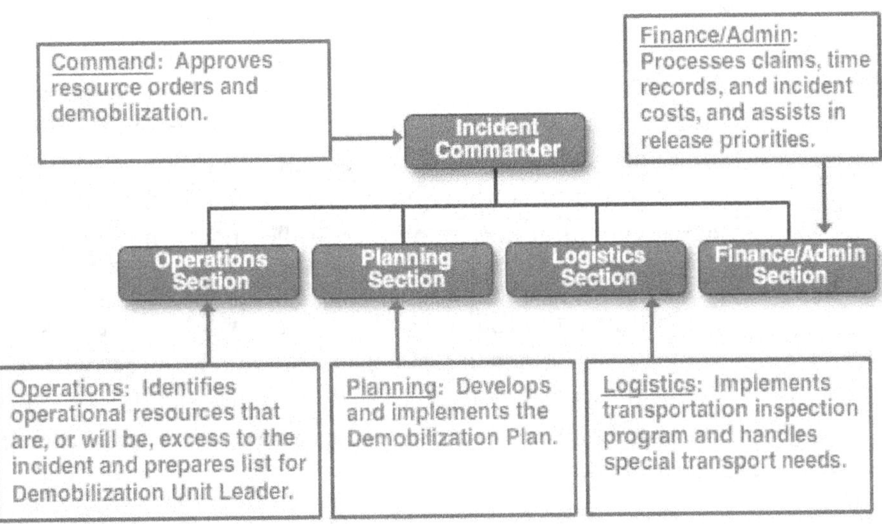

Early Demobilization Planning

Managers should plan and prepare for the demobilization process at the same time that they begin the resource mobilization process. Early planning for demobilization facilitates accountability and makes the transportation of resources as efficient as possible—in terms of both costs and time of delivery. Indicators that the incident may be ready to implement a demobilization plan include:

- Fewer resource requests being received.
- More resources spending more time in staging.
- Excess resources identified during planning process.
- Incident objectives have been accomplished.

After the incident is controlled, and tactical resources are beginning to be released, the incident management organization should begin to monitor the number of support and management staff that are assigned. Below are some typical workload considerations to consider when planning for demobilization.

Position	Demobilization Considerations
Public Information Officer	Press interest may taper off toward the end of the incident, especially when tactics turn from life safety to cleanup. As the incident demobilizes, the need for interagency coordination of information may also decline. While it is important that the press continue to have a contact at the incident, it may be possible for the Public Information Officer to scale back operations.
Safety Officer	As the number of tactical operations at an incident decreases, the demand on the Safety Officer will also decline. However, some incidents require post-incident debriefings that will require the input of the Safety Officer. While the workload may level out, it may remain until the end of the incident.
Liaison Officer	As Cooperating and Assisting Agency resources are demobilized, the Liaison Officer's job will become less complex. The Liaison Officer is also likely to be involved in interagency post-incident review activities that may require continued presence at the incident and involvement after final demobilization.
Operations Section	The Operations Section Chief should be able to reduce support staff such as Deputies and Staging Area Managers as the Operations Section is demobilized.
Planning Section	In the Planning Section, the later workload falls on the Demobilization and Documentation Units. The Demobilization Unit will develop the Demobilization Plan and monitor its implementation. The Documentation Unit will package all incident documentation for archiving with the responsible agency or jurisdiction. Both of these processes are finished late in the incident.
Logistics Section	The Supply Unit and the Facilities Unit play major roles as the incident winds down. The Facilities Unit will need to demobilize the incident facilities, such as the command post and incident base. The Supply Unit must collect, inventory, and arrange to refurbish, rehabilitate, or replace resources depleted, lost, or damaged at the incident.
Finance and Administration Section	Many of the activities of the Finance and Administration Section continue well after the rest of the organization has been demobilized. Much of the paperwork needed to document an incident is completed during or after demobilization.

Incident Demobilization: Safety and Cost

When planning to demobilize resources, consideration must be given to:

- **Safety.** Organizations should watch for "first in, last out" syndrome. Resources that were first on scene should be considered for early release. Also, these resources should be evaluated for fatigue and the distance they will need to travel to their home base prior to release.
- **Cost.** Expensive resources should be monitored carefully to ensure that they are released as soon as they are no longer needed, or if their task can be accomplished in a more cost-effective manner.

Developing a Written Demobilization Plan

A formal demobilization process and plan should be developed when personnel:

- Have traveled a long distance and/or require commercial transportation.
- Are fatigued, causing potential safety issues.
- Should receive medical and/or stress management debriefings.
- Are required to complete task books or other performance evaluations.
- Need to contribute to the after-action review and identification of lessons learned.

In addition, written demobilization plans are useful when there is equipment that needs to be serviced or have safety checks performed.

Incident Demobilization: Release Priorities

Agencies will differ in how they establish release priorities for resources assigned to an incident. An example of release priorities might be (in order of release):

- Contracted or commercial resources.
- Mutual aid and assistance resources.
- First-in agency resources.
- Resources needed for cleanup or rehabilitation.

Agency policies, procedures, and agreements must be considered by the incident management prior to releasing resources. For example, if the drivers of large vehicles carry special licenses (commercial rating, for example), they may be affected by local, tribal, State, and Federal regulations for the amount of rest required before a driver can get back on the road.

Demobilization Accountability

Incident personnel are considered under incident management and responsibility until they reach their home base or new assignment. In some circumstances this may also apply to contracted resources. For reasons of liability, it is important that the incident organization mitigate potential safety issues (such as fatigue) prior to letting resources depart for home.

On large incidents, especially those which may have personnel and tactical resources from several jurisdictions or agencies, and where there has been an extensive integration of multijurisdiction or agency personnel into the incident organization, a Demobilization Unit within the Planning Section should be established early in the life of the incident. A written demobilization plan is essential on larger incidents.

Step 6: Reimburse

Reimbursement provides a mechanism to recoup funds expended for incident-specific activities. Consideration should be given to reimbursement agreements prior to an incident.

Processes for reimbursement play an important role in establishing and maintaining the readiness of resources.

Reimbursement Terms and Arrangements

Preparedness plans, mutual aid agreements, and assistance agreements should specify reimbursement terms and arrangements for:

- Collecting bills and documentation.
- Validating costs against the scope of the work.
- Ensuring that proper authorities are secured.
- Using proper procedures/forms and accessing any reimbursement software programs.

Step 7: Inventory

Resource management uses various resource inventory systems to assess the availability of assets provided by jurisdictions.

The previous lesson covered the preparedness activities of resource typing and credentialing.

Credentialing: The credentialing process entails the objective evaluation and documentation of an individual's current certification, license, or degree; training and experience; and competence or proficiency to meet nationally accepted standards, provide particular services and/or functions, or perform specific tasks under specific conditions during an incident.

Resource Typing: Resource typing is categorizing, by capability, the resources requested, deployed, and used in incidents. Measurable standards identifying resource capabilities and performance levels serve as the basis for categories. Resource users at all levels use these standards to identify and inventory resources. Resource kinds may be divided into subcategories to define more precisely the capabilities needed to meet specific requirements. Resource typing is a continuous process designed to be as simple as possible; it facilitates frequent use and accuracy in obtaining needed resources.

Maintaining Current Data

Preparedness organizations should inventory and maintain current data on their available resources. The data are then made available to communications/dispatch centers, Emergency Operations Centers, and other organizations within the Multiagency Coordination System.

Resources identified within an inventory system are not an indication of automatic availability. The jurisdiction and/or owner of the resources have the final determination on availability.

Inventory Systems

Inventory systems for resource management should be adaptable and scalable and should account for the potential of double-counting personnel and/or equipment. In particular, resource summaries should clearly reflect any overlap of personnel across different resource pools. Personnel inventories should reflect single resources with multiple skills, taking care not to overstate the total resources.

For example, many firefighters also have credentials as emergency medical technicians (EMTs). A resource summary, then, could count a firefighter as a firefighter or as an EMT, but not as both. The total should reflect the number of available personnel, not simply the sum of the firefighter and EMT counts.

Lesson 5:

Resource Management & Complex Incidents

Characteristics of Complex Incidents

Complex incidents are those beyond business as usual. Their characteristics may include most, if not all, of those listed below:

- Involve more than one agency (often many)
- May involve more than one political jurisdiction
- Have the most complex management and communication problems
- Require more experienced, qualified supervisory personnel
- Require the long-term commitment of large numbers of tactical and support resources
- Cause more injury, illness, and death
- Produce the most damage to property and the environment
- Have extreme elements of crisis/psychological trauma that diminish human capacity to function
- Last longer
- Are the most costly to control
- Require extensive mitigation, recovery, and rehabilitation
- Have greater media interest
- May require management of volunteers and donations, both solicited and unsolicited

Coordinating Resources

The process for coordinating resources for complex incidents dovetails with that used for individual, smaller incidents. However, most of the action takes place within the entities that comprise the Multiagency Coordination (MAC) System. Elements of MAC Systems may include:

- Local, State, and Federal Emergency Operations Centers (EOCs).
- MAC System Groups.
- FEMA Regional Response Coordination Centers.
- Joint Field Offices (JFOs).
- National Response Framework agencies.

- Department of Homeland Security.

It must be remembered that the authority and structure of EOCs, MAC System elements, etc., varies from agency to agency and jurisdiction to jurisdiction. However, it is important also to remember the difference between command and coordination.

Command and Coordination

The Incident Management Team (IMT) has authority for **command** of the incident. This authority is delegated directly from the Agency Administrator. The Incident Management Team determines incident objectives and tactics, and assigns resources to carry them out. The MAC System is responsible for **coordinating** support to the incident(s). This may include prioritizing incidents for the purpose of allocating scarce resources, mobilizing resources, ensuring interagency and interjurisdictional coordination, and making policy decisions to support incidents, but not decisions reserved for Area Commands and Incident Commanders.

Coordinating Resource Needs: Step 1

The first step in coordinating resource needs is a thorough assessment or "sizeup" of the current incident situation and future incident potential. The scope and details of this assessment depend on the jurisdictional level of the organization. For example, a County EOC must have a detailed understanding of the status of all jurisdictions and current incidents within its purview, plus a good understanding of the status of surrounding counties. The EOC should also maintain a general awareness of national conditions, especially for situations that may affect resource availability.

EOC Manager

As you can see, we are in the direct path of the hurricane that came on shore this morning. We are paying close attention to what is happening to the counties between us and the storm, hoping it will give us an idea of the amount of damage we can expect. We are also in close contact with the counties directly around us, and with those through which our evacuation passes. It wouldn't do to have our evacuees run into someone else's roadblocks! I'm also concerned about the region, because it will affect State and national resource availability.

Coordinating Resource Needs: Step 2

The Incident Commander develops incident objectives. For the supporting coordination entities, these objectives may translate into requests for additional resources. One of the characteristics of complex incidents is that there may be competition for limited critical resources.

In order to allocate resources appropriately, the MAC System must be able to prioritize multiple incidents happening simultaneously.

Life safety is always the first priority when making resource allocation decisions.

Coordinating Resource Needs: Steps 3 and 4

Step 3:

Allocate scarce resources according to priority.

Step 4:

Determine additional steps that need to be taken. These additional steps could include mission-tasking other organizations for resources, making policy decisions to assist in the response, allocating donated goods and services, etc. For example, in Incident #4 in the activity just completed, there may be ways to accomplish the security and traffic control needs at the hospital without assigning sworn police officers. Many event management companies have employees experienced in crowd and traffic control and security.

Mobilizing Resources

During complex incidents, resource mobilization becomes complicated, as more agencies and levels of government become involved, more incidents require assistance, supply lines and response times get longer, and more resources mobilize. This increased workload is often underestimated.

Maintaining ordering discipline and the coordination chain will assist in avoiding duplication of effort, additional expense, and lost requests. However, it is important to remember that, in some complex incidents, State and Federal resources may take some time to arrive.

The Incident Command/Unified Command identifies resource requirements and communicates needs through the Area Command (if established) to the local Emergency Operations Center (EOC). The local EOC fulfills the need or requests assistance through mutual aid agreements and assistance agreements with private-sector and nongovernmental organizations.

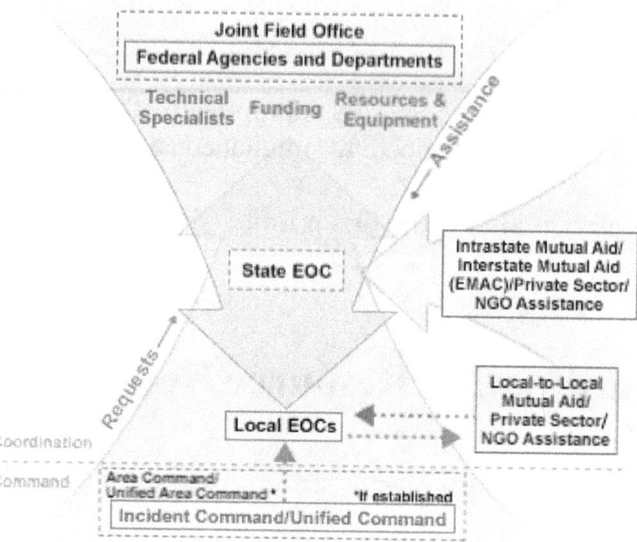

In most incidents, local resources and local mutual aid and assistance agreements will provide the first line of emergency response and incident management. If the State cannot meet the needs, they may arrange support from another State through an agreement, such as the Emergency Management Assistance Compact (EMAC), or through assistance agreements with nongovernmental organizations.

If additional resources and/or capabilities are required beyond those available through interstate agreements, the Governor may ask the President for Federal assistance.

The Joint Field Office is used to manage Federal assistance (technical specialists, funding, and resources/equipment) that is made available based on the specifics and magnitude of the incident. In instances when an incident is projected to have catastrophic implications (e.g., a major hurricane or flooding), States and/or the Federal Government may position resources in the anticipated incident area.

In cases where there is time to assess the requirements and plan for a catastrophic incident, the Federal response will be coordinated with State, tribal, and local jurisdictions, and the pre-positioning of Federal assets will be tailored to address the specific situation.

*Note that some Federal agencies (U.S. Coast Guard, Environmental Protection Agency, etc.) have statutory responsibility for response and may coordinate and/or integrate directly with affected jurisdictions.

Dealing With Convergence

Convergence is the result of unstructured response to an incident. Convergence can come from several sources, and may severely hamper incident response activities, as well as place an enormous logistical burden on an already burdened system. It may also provide unexpected benefits, especially in the period of time between the occurrence of the incident and the arrival of State and Federal resources.

Convergence issues may include any or all of the following:

- Local resources (requested resources, and also well-intentioned freelancing and self-dispatched emergency responders)
- State and Federal agency resources (requested resources, as well as self-dispatched resources from field offices close to the incident)
- Donations and volunteer assistance
- VIP visits

Emergency Responder Convergence

Even under "normal" incident conditions, the incident scene can rapidly become clogged with apparatus, command staff vehicles, and bystanders. Such congestion:

- Causes unnecessary exposure to hazards (including incidents where responders may be the primary or secondary target).
- Makes access difficult for resources that are needed for the response.
- Complicates resource accountability and tracking.

During major events, this "normal" congestion can become aggravated by self-dispatched and freelancing emergency responders. Self-dispatched resources and freelancing cause serious problems. Personnel should NOT respond to the scene unless requested or dispatched.

In addition to creating the problems noted earlier, emergency responder convergence may:

- Deplete reserve resources that are needed to provide continued services to the community.
- Compromise service provided under mutual aid and assistance agreements and disrupt orderly backup/moveup coverage.
- Make it impossible to track resources or maintain resource accountability.
- Interfere with evacuation.
- Hamper access of formally requested resources.
- Make it impossible to protect responders from additional threats.

Strategies for Dealing With Emergency Responder Convergence

Strategies for dealing with responder convergence include:

- Developing a local and regional capability to augment and sustain a reinforced response for at least 72 hours. This capability should be accompanied by policies governing self-dispatch and freelancing. Self-dispatch may be unavoidable—even necessary under certain extreme conditions—and should be part of the planning process.
- Developing a plan for continued public safety service. This plan should include an organized policy and procedure for the orderly recall of additional personnel, as well as a policy to define the deployment of personnel to assist other agencies in times of crisis. Don't forget to include backup for EOC personnel as well as emergency responders and ICS staff.
- Establishing and enforcing inner and outer perimeters. Exclude freelancing or self-dispatched resources as well as unauthorized civilian or volunteer access.
- Establishing and enforcing a controlled access plan for authorized personnel. This may require immediate access to large quantities of fencing materials.
- Developing, establishing, and enforcing a coordinated traffic management and evacuation plan.
- Establishing and enforcing Staging Areas.

Lessons Learned: Emergency Responder Convergence

All three jurisdictions responding to the 9/11 attacks faced freelancing emergency responders from the home agency and from nearby mutual aid cooperators. As a result of this, the New York Fire Department has implemented the following policies:

- Only on-duty members shall respond to alarms on apparatus.
- Persons other than members of the New York Fire Department are to be excluded from the response. This includes former members of the department, members of other fire departments, friends, and relatives.
- Members who have arrived at incidents prior to responding companies, and those whose assistance has been accepted by authorized Fire Officers, are subject to the direction and control of the Incident Commander. It is the policy of the department that such members are relieved as soon as sufficient on-duty, properly equipped and protected resources have arrived. The Incident Commander's authority in this matter is absolute.
- In response to recall, members shall report to their assigned quarters. They shall not respond directly to the incident.

State and National Mobilizations

While interstate Emergency Management Assistance Compacts (EMAC system) and the National Response Framework provide vital resources to overwhelmed jurisdictions, their arrival can cause additional convergence issues. Even resources such as Urban Search and Rescue (US&R) Task Forces, who come prepared to be self-sufficient for 72 hours, will need a secure location in which to store equipment, conduct planning, eat, and sleep. Other teams, such as a Disaster Mortuary Team (DMORT) or National Transportation Safety Board (NTSB) accident investigation teams, may need specific kinds of support from local government, including special facilities and utility needs, and security assistance.

In order to be able to deploy immediately, most Federal resources arrive with a full contingent of personnel, equipment, and supplies. A review of the components of the FEMA US&R Task Forces reveals how significant the amount of resources may be.

Strategies for State and National Deployments

Strategies for managing State and national deployments include:

- Making sure that statewide mutual aid agreements include instructions on staging, standards for ensuring interoperability of equipment and communication, the expected degree of self-sufficiency, and the specific support expected from the host jurisdiction.
- Reviewing and assessing the support requirements of frequently deployed national resources.
- Developing a plan to integrate State and Federal assets into incident operations. Plan for the use of Unified Command and interdisciplinary tactical operations.
- Building relationships with State and Federal officials likely to respond to complex incidents by training and exercising together.
- Identifying locations suitable for remote Staging Areas, Incident Bases, Receiving and Distribution Centers, and Mobilization Centers.

It is important to preidentify facilities necessary to support State and Federal mobilizations.

- Facilities will be required for the incident itself, including the Incident Command Post, Staging Areas (run by Operations), and Incident Bases (managed by Logistics).
- Facilities are also needed "off-incident," such as Receiving and Distribution and Mobilization/Demobilization Centers, where resources are gathered, housed, and supported while awaiting specific incident assignments, and locations for Disaster

Recovery Centers (DRCs), Joint Operations Centers (JOCs), and Joint Information Centers (JICs).

In addition to the facilities themselves, resource considerations should include:

- Security.
- Parking.
- Access.
- Utilities.
- Access to commercial sources of food, sanitation, lodging.
- Janitorial and garbage service.

Donations and Volunteer Assistance

It is difficult to overstate the monetary and psychological importance of donations and volunteer assistance during a major disaster. Successfully managing and tracking donations and coordinating the efforts of volunteers (solicited or unsolicited) can be a significant political, psychological, and logistical opportunity—and a problem.

Donations take the form of either funds, or donations of goods and services. The key to successful management of these assets is having a preincident plan for soliciting, gathering, prioritizing, and distributing appropriate donations.

The system must also be prepared to deal with inappropriate donations without bogging down the distribution of essential goods and services.

The inability to manage donations can lead to an "emergency within an emergency." It may even become necessary for the jurisdiction to protect itself from charges of mismanagement, or from being billed at a later date for goods and services presented as "donations" at the time.

Strategies for Dealing With Donations

Strategies for managing donations include:

- Consulting with organizations that are used to soliciting, managing, and distributing donated goods and funds.
- Developing and training volunteer resources to assist with donations and volunteer management.
- Developing public information and media releases that provide direction for those who wish to donate.

- Developing and implementing an effective management structure to receive, warehouse, inventory, organize, distribute, and account for large-scale donations.

Unaffiliated Volunteers

Unaffiliated volunteers, also known as spontaneous volunteers, are individuals who offer to help or self-deploy to assist in emergency situations without fully coordinating their activities. These volunteers are considered "unaffiliated" in that they are not part of a disaster relief organization.

Unaffiliated volunteers can be significant resources, but because they do not have preestablished relationships with emergency response organizations, verifying their training or credentials and matching them with the appropriate service areas can be difficult.

Strategies for Managing Volunteers

The first strategy for managing volunteers is to establish working relationships with the local organizations representing these entities:

- **National Voluntary Organizations Active in Disaster (National VOAD)** is the forum where organizations share knowledge and resources throughout the disaster cycle—preparation, response, and recovery—to help disaster survivors and their communities. National VOAD members are the primary coordinating nonprofit organizations for the management of unaffiliated volunteers.
- **Citizen Corps** helps coordinate volunteer activities that will make our communities safer, stronger, and better prepared to respond to any emergency situation. It provides opportunities for people to participate in a range of measures to make their families, their homes, and their communities safer from the threats of crime, terrorism, and disasters of all kinds.

Volunteers such as amateur radio operators, search and rescue teams, CERTs, police and fire auxiliaries, and reserves are valued members of emergency management organizations in many jurisdictions.

Such resources are known quantities that train and exercise to play specific roles in an incident. These volunteers have long-standing formal relationships that are spelled out in written agreements and standard operating procedures. Individual members have credentials and identification issued by the volunteer organization itself and/or the emergency management organization with which it has the agreement.

Consider:

- Developing a CERT capability if your jurisdiction does not have one.
- Making sure agreements with volunteer organizations clearly spell out required training, experience, and equipment, as well as liability and employment relationship to the jurisdiction.
- Developing and implementing an effective management structure to receive spontaneous volunteers, catalog their skills, provide on-the-job training, deploy, and supervise activities.
- Developing public information and media releases that provide direction for those who wish to volunteer.

VIP Visits

VIP visits cause yet another convergence issue for incidents. Depending on who the visitors are and where they want to go, these visits can disrupt incident operations, cause additional traffic congestion, and attract a larger media presence.

On the other hand, such visits are valuable in providing VIPs with a realistic view of the problems posed by the disaster, and they may result in enhanced resources and provide a morale boost to responders and survivors. Most VIPs are aware of the impact their presence may have on operations, and are willing to coordinate visits with the incident management organization.

Strategies for Dealing With VIP Visits

Strategies for dealing with VIP visits include the following:

- When possible, encourage such visitors to wait until after the 72-hour window for successful rescues has passed.
- If visits must be scheduled before then, attempt to schedule visits to less time-sensitive operations.
- Identify appropriate background shots, photo opportunities, etc., before the visit.
- Confirm availability of key personnel (Public Information Officers, Incident Commanders, etc.) prior to the VIP's arrival.

Try to limit time spent on scene. Conduct business away from the scene if possible.

Self-Dispatched Resources

The use of self-dispatched resources is highly discouraged. If your incident assigns a resource outside of the normal activation and request process, it is possible that your agency or jurisdiction may become liable for their actions, or for any accidents or injuries they incur while working. Your agency or jurisdiction may also be responsible for any expenses or reimbursement.

Although these resources may be trained and capable, the risks associated with assigning self-dispatched resources outweigh the advantages.

Strategies for Dealing With Self-Dispatched Resources

If self-dispatched resources must be used, consider the following strategies:

- Self-dispatched resources may become freelancers if the incident organization cannot organize to use them. Instruct perimeter personnel to refer self-dispatched emergency resources to staging or mobilization points. Staging Area Managers and Resource Unit Check-In Recorders must be ready to inventory resources for skills and readiness, check them in, organize them into appropriate tactical configurations and assign them to the incident. If their skills are not needed, they should return to normal status to avoid unnecessary impact on overall public safety coverage.
- A self-dispatched resource that has been accepted and assigned to the incident must be included in the resource tracking and incident planning process.
- Information about the resource should be shared with the rest of the Command and General Staff, especially the Liaison Officer, and the Planning, Logistics, and Finance/Administration Section Chiefs.
- Nongovernmental and private-sector resources should be inspected and formal agreements completed as soon as possible.
- The presence and status of public-sector resources on the incident should be reported to their home agency.